Lecture Notes
in Business Information Processing   457

Series Editors

Wil van der Aalst ⓘ
  RWTH Aachen University, Aachen, Germany

John Mylopoulos ⓘ
  University of Trento, Trento, Italy

Sudha Ram ⓘ
  University of Arizona, Tucson, AZ, USA

Michael Rosemann ⓘ
  Queensland University of Technology, Brisbane, QLD, Australia

Clemens Szyperski
  Microsoft Research, Redmond, WA, USA

More information about this series at https://link.springer.com/bookseries/7911

Eduard Babkin · Joseph Barjis ·
Pavel Malyzhenkov · Vojtěch Merunka (Eds.)

Model-Driven Organizational and Business Agility

Second International Workshop, MOBA 2022
Leuven, Belgium, June 6–7, 2022
Revised Selected Papers

Springer

Editors
Eduard Babkin ⓘ
National Research University, Higher School
of Economics
Nizhny Novgorod, Russia

Pavel Malyzhenkov ⓘ
National Research University, Higher School
of Economics
Nizhny Novgorod, Russia

Joseph Barjis
San Jose State University
San Jose, CA, USA

Vojtěch Merunka ⓘ
Czech Technical University in Prague
Prague, Czech Republic

ISSN 1865-1348   ISSN 1865-1356 (electronic)
Lecture Notes in Business Information Processing
ISBN 978-3-031-17727-9   ISBN 978-3-031-17728-6 (eBook)
https://doi.org/10.1007/978-3-031-17728-6

This Springer imprint is published by the registered company Springer Nature Switzerland AG
The registered company address is: Gewerbestrasse 11, 6330 Cham, Switzerland

Preface

The current reality in the corporate world demands enterprises to be agile in every aspect. This implies agility as an organization, agility in responding to changes, and agility in strategy and execution. All this culminates in agility in delivering products (solutions) to the customer, which has fostered development of a myriad of agile frameworks and agile development approaches. However, agile practice is often driven by mere pragmatics and relevance, that is, applying agile with little research and, often, little rigor. This presents opportunities for researchers to look at the agile field through the lens of research and bring more rigor to it.

The experience of recent years shows that software engineering or any system development has an essential intersection with business engineering, management consulting, customer engagement, and many more. This makes modern software or any system development a cross-functional activity, and this recognition brings software engineering beyond merely writing program code. In fact, agile practice emphasizes that requirements emerge as the software system goes through the development process. Agile practice does not even assume that the requirements must be completely and accurately identified at the beginning of the development life cycle, but rather continuously explored.

The International Workshop on Model-driven Organizational and Business Agility (MOBA) was launched in 2021 with the purpose of encouraging scientific inquiries into agile practice and agility in a wider context, that is, an entire enterprise. In doing so, the role of models and modeling was especially taken into the focus.

The central tenet of an agile mindset is to develop a capability to rapidly respond to changes and to reduce uncertainty by iteratively exploring the solution context and scope and incrementally delivering value to the customer. In this sense, agile practice has equal merit whether developing an IT application, i.e., software engineering, or non-IT functions such as marketing, operations, human resources, legal work, etc. However, in its current state, agile practice is predominantly applied in the IT domain as it is applied in all stages of the life cycle of modern IT systems. As such, only a fraction of the true potential that agile practice can bring to enterprises is utilized. Therefore, the vast unexplored opportunities and the corresponding stasis in agile practice would greatly benefit from scientific inquiry, research, and rigorous solutions.

To explore these opportunities and address the potential challenges, the MOBA workshop aims at developing a multi-disciplinary community of researchers and practitioners, which will consolidate the effort in detecting, modeling, improving, and disseminating rigorous agility practices and theories. In this regard, various agility phenomena will be studied from a systemic viewpoint, distinguishing between endogenous agility inside an organization and exogenous agility in the form business connections with external parties. Common principles of model-driven research and engineering of organizational or technical artefacts will guarantee consistency and interoperability of the results obtained.

To model and study organizational and business agility in a system context we inevitably should join together many adjacent topics such as enterprise architecture, semantic interoperability, model-driven design of information systems, models validation, business value co-creation, and more.

As a community, MOBA aims to become an incubator and platform for nascent and innovative ideas that are in their infancy and need expert discussion, insights, and critical evaluation by peers. In this sense, MOBA facilitates the participation and success of junior researchers. This year, MOBA continued its Master and Doctoral Consortium, which attracted young researchers to present and discuss their work, and receive feedback and inspiration from peers.

MOBA 2022 was held in conjunction with the 34th International Conference on Advanced Information Systems Engineering (CAiSE 2022) and took place during June 6–7, 2022. The workshop received 22 submissions, and each paper underwent triple-blind peer reviews by 3 members of the Program Committee. As a result, 10 papers were accepted for presentation at the workshop and publication in this proceedings volume. In addition, one keynote paper is included.

The MOBA 2022 organizers would like to express their sincere thanks to the emerging MOBA community: the authors, the Program Committee, and the CAiSE organizers and chairs for their enthusiasm and devotion, as well as all participants for their contributions. We are already looking forward to the next edition of MOBA to meet again and bring new researchers!

June 2022   Eduard Babkin
Joseph Barjis
Pavel Malyzhenkov
Vojtěch Merunka

Organization

MOBA 2022 was organized in cooperation with CAiSE 2022 (Leuven, Belgium).

Executive Committee

General Chair

Eduard Babkin   National Research University Higher School of Economics, Nizhny Novgorod, Russia

Program Chairs

Joseph Barjis	San Jose State University, USA
Pavel Malyzhenkov	National Research University Higher School of Economics, Nizhny Novgorod, Russia
Vojtech Merunka	Czech Technical University in Prague and Czech University of Life Sciences, Czech Republic

Program Committee

Eduard Babkin	National Research University Higher School of Economics, Nizhni Novgorod, Russia
Joseph Barjis	San Jose State University, USA
Anna Bobkowska	Gdansk University of Technology, Poland
Alexander Bock	University of Duisburg-Essen, Germany
Luiz Olavo Bonino	University of Twente, The Netherlands
Mahmoud Boufaida	Frères Mentouri University of Constantine, Algeria
Peter de Bruyn	University of Antwerp, Belgium
Simona Colucci	Politecnico di Bari, Italy
Francesco M. Donini	University of Tuscia, Italy
Samuel Fosso Wamba	Toulouse Business School, France
Sergio Guerreiro	Instituto Superior Tecnico, University of Lisbon, Portugal
Giancarlo Guizzardi	Free University of Bozen-Bolzano, Italy
Georg Grossmann	UniSA STEM, Australia
Kristina Hettne	Leiden University, The Netherlands
Frantisek Hunka	University of Ostrava, Czech Republic
Rossi Kamal	Kyung Hee University, South Korea

Contents

Invited Paper

Workshop Papers

Cross-Pollination of Personas, User Stories, Use Cases and Business-Process Models

Peter Forbrig[✉] and Anke Dittmar

Department of Computer Science, Chair in Software Engineering, University of Rostock,
Albert-Einstein-Str.22, 18059 Rostock, Germany
{peter.forbrig,anke.dittmar}@uni-rostock.de

Abstract. Agile process management also requires an agile development of business-process specifications. The paper discusses at the example of user stories, use-case slices, personas and subject-oriented business models how concepts of an integrated use of models in user-centered and agile software development can be transferred to business-process modeling. In particular, it is suggested to map subjects of subject-oriented business models to small sets of personas with related user stories to facilitate more expressive behavioral specifications. The user stories can be derived from current and envisaged scenarios that support the communication in enterprises. The proposed splitting of subjects into sub-roles with their specific behaviors makes possible to define slices and to increase the flexibility of process specifications. The ideas are illustrated through an example.

Keywords: User stories · Personas · Business process models · S-BPM · Subjects and sub-roles · Behavioral models · Use-case slices · User-centered development

1 Introduction

Communication between stakeholders is crucial for understanding and describing requirements of software systems and for business-process modelling. User-centered design approaches emphasize in this context the active involvement of diverse stakeholders and the need of models and design representations which can be easily understood and support a mutual understanding of the design problem. Agile practices which are now common in software development prefer flexible modeling approaches and notations such as user stories which facilitate quick responses to changing needs of customers.

While the need for agile process management in companies is acknowledged, there has been relatively little work on the agile development of business-process specifications themselves. This paper investigates how ideas about a flexible and shared use of models in user-centered and agile software development can inform the business-process model development. In particular, we look at a combined use of stories, personas, use case slices and subject-oriented business process models (S-BPM). According to Fleischmann et al. [15], S-BPM specifications can especially good handle agile process management. The S-BPM language consisting of only a limited number of elements was designed to enable domain experts to specify by themselves the business processes.

© The Author(s), under exclusive license to Springer Nature Switzerland AG 2022
E. Babkin et al. (Eds.): MOBA 2022, LNBIP 457, pp. 3–18, 2022.
https://doi.org/10.1007/978-3-031-17728-6_1

Stories are generally considered to be an important means for knowledge transfer and sense-making processes. They have become a management tool for companies [25]. In user-centered design, stories are used to reflect on current and envisaged practices and to support design decisions. User stories in agile software development are informal descriptions of requirements from the perspective of certain user roles. These different understandings and uses of stories have to be better understood.

This paper discusses how the different types of stories might be usefully combined. Stories in user-centered design are deeply related to personas. User stories can be seen as "agile use cases" but with less precise descriptions of the interaction between the actors and the system under consideration. In previous work, we explored an integrated use of personas and use cases [11]. While use cases help to consider a system from the perspective of users acting in certain roles, the additional use of personas (implemented, for example, by use case slices) help to distinguish between different user groups and to deliver more expressive but still compact behavioral specifications. In this paper, we apply similar ideas to business-process models in S-BPM [17] and BPMN [4]. As far as we are aware of, the concept of personas was not used in connection to business-process modelling beforehand.

The paper is structured as follows. Section 2 provides some background on above mentioned models from the different fields of interaction design, software engineering, and business process modelling. In Sect. 3, possible combinations of different versions of stories and personas with process models are discussed in combination with an example for managing business trips. The paper closes with a discussion and a summary.

2   Background and Related Work

This section introduces the main ideas of the various forms of stories used in software development and business process modelling, use cases with use-case slices, and personas. The notation for subject-oriented business process management is briefly presented.

2.1   User Stories

Originally, the term user story was introduced in the context of interaction design. Later the term was used in agile software development but with a different understanding as shown later.

According to Quesenbery and Brooks [28] "[s]tories have always been part of user experience design as scenarios, storyboard, flow charts, personas, and every other technique that we use to communicate how (and why) a new design will work. As a part of user experience design, stories serve to ground the work in a real context by connecting design ideas to the people who will use the product". The authors identify five advantages of user stories:

1. They help to gather and share information about users, tasks, and goals.
2. They put a human face on analytic data.
3. They can spark new design concepts and encourage collaboration and innovation.

4. They help to understand the world by giving us insight into people who are different.
5. They can even persuade others of the value of a contribution.

User stories in interaction design are typically narratives with an introduction, middle part and ending part. They help to describe the design problem and the application context of the system under design in a way that evokes the empathy of the analysts and developers. Stories about current and envisaged situations support the reflection upon consequences of design alternatives, and thus support design decisions (e.g., for functional requirements). Rosson and Carroll [30] in their scenario-based design approach [30] use the terms problem scenario and activity scenario for narrative descriptions of current and envisioned usage episodes and suggest to develop them together with claims to explore problem and design spaces.

Stories could be employed in a similar way to reflect upon new business-process models and their consequences for a company.

In the context of business administration, Thiel [32] refers to the potential of stories for reaching customer and employee loyalty. Fog et al. [16] use storytelling as management tool and state: "The stories we share with others are the building blocks of any human relationship. Stories place our shared experiences in words and images. They help shape our perception of "who we are" and "what we stand for". Likewise, stories are told and flow through all companies".

Denning [10] provides eight different story patterns.

1. Sparking action	2. Communicate who you are
3. Transmitting values	4. Communicating your brand
5. Fostering Collaboration	6. Taming the grapevine
7. Sharing knowledge	8. Leading people into the future

The Sparking action pattern describes how a successful change was implemented in the past, but allows listeners to imagine how it might work in their situation. For transmitting values, Denning recommends to use believable characters and situations. The brand is usually told by the product or service itself. To foster collaboration, the stories should recount situations that listeners have experienced. They should be animated to share their own stories. Taming the grapevine refers to storytelling with gentle humor about some aspect of a rumor that reveals it to be untrue. Sharing knowledge focuses on problems and how they were corrected. The story should have an explanation of why the solution worked. Leading people into the future evokes the future that is planned to be created.

In agile software development, the term "user story" has quite a different semantics. Here, a user story consists of one sentence with the following structure.

As a <role>, I want <feature> so that <reason>.

The following two sentences provide examples of such stories.

• *As an employee, I want to upload messages so that I can share them with others.*

- *As an administrator, I want to approve messages before they are posted so that I can make sure they are appropriate.*

User stories in agile software development basically describe functional requirements from the perspective of a role. They are employed by software developers to derive their tasks for implementing the system under discussion. User stories can be specified on different levels of abstractions. Lawrence and Green [24] provide nine patterns for spitting user stories (workflow steps, operations, business rule variation, variations in data, break out spike, interface variations, major effort, simple/complex, and defer performance). In each pattern, conditions for its application and resulting actions are described. For instance, the workflow step pattern can be applied to the following user story as discussed in [24]:

- *As a content manager, I can publish a news story to the corporate website.*

The authors comment on the example: "It turned out that just to get a few sentence news story on the corporate website required both editorial and legal approval and final review on a staging site. There's no way 6–10 stories like this would fit in an iteration. In a workflow like this, the biggest value often comes from the beginning and end. The middle steps add incremental value, but don't stand alone. So, it can work well to build the simple end-to-end case first and then add the middle steps and special cases." [24]. Hence, the story was split into several stories:

1. As a content manager, I can publish a news story directly to the corporate website.
2. As a content manager, I can publish a news story with editor review.
3. As a content manager, I can publish a news story with legal review.
4. As a content manager, I can view a news story on a staging site.
5. As a content manager, I can publish a news story from the staging site to production.

The workflow steps pattern stimulates developers to think about variants of task or business-process execution. We will focus on this kind of user stories in the paper because they are very much related to use cases and use-case slices, which are discussed in the next subsection.

2.2 Use Cases and Use-Case Slices

Use cases are models that focus on the functional aspect of a software system and describe it as it appears to users. They were introduced by Jacobson (see e.g. [20]) and "represent the things of value that the system performs for its actors" [2].

A use case diagram gives an overview about the system under consideration in terms of primary actors (representing users, or more precisely, user roles), use cases (representing user goals), and secondary actors (representing external services employed by the system). Use case diagrams found their way into the unified modeling language UML (an example diagram is shown in Fig. 2). However, they should be enriched with textual specifications of each use case to understand and describe more precisely the interactions between users and systems. The metaphor of a book is often used in this context. The diagram has the role of the outline and the structured texts have the role of the different chapters.

There are diverse formats for textual use case specifications. Cockburn's [8] template is one of the most used templates though. It recommends to define for each use case a title, goal, primary actor, level, precondition, main success scenario, alternative scenarios etc. Use cases are considered here to be sets of scenarios. The main success scenario describes a sequence of actions (steps) of the system and the primary actor which lead to the achievement of the goal. Alternative scenarios describe deviations from the main success scenario in exceptional or failure situations.

Sometimes use cases are very complex and it might take several months to implement them. This does not fit to agile development having implementation sprints of about four weeks. Therefore, Jacobson et al. [21, 22] adapted use cases by introducing the concept of use-case slices for Use Case 2.0.

In UseCase 2.0, the authors refer to the above mentioned scenarios as stories. In other words, stories in the terminology of Use Case 2.0 are sequences of actions. A use-case slice contains now those stories (scenarios) which have to be implemented in a single sprint. It "is created by selecting one or more stories for implementation..., acts as a placeholder for all the work required to complete the implementation of the stories..., and evolves to include the equivalent slices through design, implementation and test" [21]. Figure 1 provides an abstract visualization of the idea of use case slices.

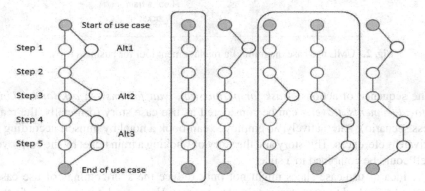

Fig. 1. Use case, use-case slices and their stories (scenarios) according to [22].

On the left-hand side of Fig. 1, all scenarios of a use case are depicted. The main success scenario is represented by the steps (circles) on the straight line. Additionally, alternative paths are sketched. On the right-hand side, possible single stories (scenarios) are indicated. One or several stories can be grouped to a use-case slice which has to be implemented in the next development iteration (sprint). The rest of the stories might be grouped to slices later on or are not intended to be supported by the software under development. They might be performed manually.

The splitting of a use case into slices looks very similar to the splitting patterns applied to user stories in agile approaches. For instance, the application of the pattern *Variations in Data* would result in similar stories like in Fig. 1.

Let us have a look at an example of a user story for a software supporting business trips that is formulated in the agile terminology.

- *As an employee, I want to get the permission of a business trip, so that everything is organized.*

A corresponding use case *Organize a trip* is indicated in the use case diagram in Fig. 2. It includes two sub use cases for booking a hotel and booking a train ticket. Besides the primary actor *Employee* there are two secondary actors. A manager has to decide about the permission of a business trip and an agent can support the booking process.

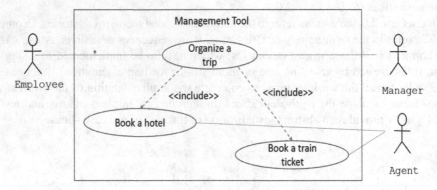

Fig. 2. UML use-case diagram of a management tool for business trips.

The sequence of actions: <*ask for permission, wait for answer, ask for booking, wait for documents, travel*> can be considered as use-case story (originally, the main success scenario). Alternatively, an employee can book a hotel by himself according to his private preferences. This story and the story of booking a train ticket by the employee himself could be combined to a slice.

The idea of use-case slices might not only reduce the shortcomings of use cases but could be applied to user stories in agile contexts. However, let us postpone further discussion to the next section and have a look at personas now.

2.3 Personas

Personas are descriptions of fictive persons that represent identified user groups of the system under consideration. They were introduced into interaction design by Cooper [9] in order increase the designers' empathy with the potential users of their products. Personas can be considered as contextual models. But the exemplary description does not only convey information about the application domain (e.g. about the users' needs, goals and task environments [3]), it supports the designer's understanding of a situation from another person's perspective and thus their creativity in problem solving. Grudin and Pruitt [19] argue that the generative nature of personas supports communication in multidisciplinary teams. Related to a persona P one can try to answer questions like: "Do you think that P would like to interact with the system in this way?" or "Is this feature necessary for P?". In the context of the management tool for business trips (see Fig. 2), for example, persona Susan (see Fig. 3) could help to raise questions about how the booking of hotels should be supported. The persona approach is successful due to the human ability to make predictions about a person's behavior based on a precise description of their backgrounds and goals [19].

Personas are typically used together with scenarios (stories). Current and envisioned usage scenarios are based on the existing user perspectives to prevent designing systems "that supposedly fit everyone but in the end, fit no one" [12].

In the literature one can find different presentations of personas ranging from simple bullet-point lists to narratives enriched with visual material. On the one hand, a persona description should not be too general in such a way that it describes almost everyone ('elastic persona' [23]). On the other hand, if it is too detailed it excludes users from the represented group [6]. The persona description that is partly indicated in Fig. 3 follows the template-like approach in [27]. Furthermore, Nielsen recommends to add information about the computer use, the workday, and the future goals of the persona. Such a persona description inspires requirements engineers and analysts.

Several authors in software engineering (SE), and in particular in requirements engineering, have recognized the potential of personas. Acuña et al. [1] state: "personas provide an understanding of the user, often overlooked in SE developments".

Susan Baker
- Employee at Great Ltd.,
- 1,77m tall, blond hair and brown eyes, athletic,
- Grew up in Bath,
- Is member of the volleyball team of her company,
- Likes to go to classical concerts and to visit museums.

Background:
Susan completed a master of business informatics. She lives in the village Lakeside and is currently responsible for the IT management at Great Ltd.
She has to travel a lot, and In case it is possible, she combines her business trips with visits to museums. Susan is sometimes annoyed about the carelessness of the company regarding the booking of hotels. There are differences in how much attention hotels pay to their environmental impact and she would prefer the more eco-friendly ones. She knows that, for some of the trips, she could also take the train instead of the car even ifi ti s more time-consuming. In her volleyball team, they have sometimes discussions aboutt his.

https://www.pexels.com

Fig. 3. Persona Susan (32) employee at Great Limited (from [17]).

Schneidewind et al. [31] identify the following challenges in requirements engineering that can be addressed with personas:

- Requirements of the users are often neglected.
- There exists insufficient communication about future users.
- Users, tasks and context of use are not thoroughly connected to the requirements of a system.

Francescomarino et al. [18], Faily [13] and Schneidewind et al. [31] suggest a better integration of user-centered design and goal-oriented requirements engineering.

In our previous work [11], we introduce an integration approach for use-case models and personas that can be applied to role-based interactive systems. Actors in use case models can be mapped to different personas describing different 'types' of users acting in the same role. The approach preserves the essential character of use cases and personas, but at the same time supports creative collaboration of different stakeholders in capturing requirements from an organizational perspective as well as from the users' perspectives. This paper applies ideas from [11] to the development of business process models.

2.4 Subject-Oriented Business Process Management

Subject-oriented business process management (S-BPM) supports a less technology-oriented approach as called for in BPM 2.0. It is characterized by Fleischmann [14] as socially executable BPM. "As organizations need to act flexible in the continuously changing landscape of the digital economy, their process work is increasingly driven by valued interactions among stakeholders." [14].

In S-BPM business processes are specified from the perspective of acting elements within the processes - the *subjects*. They represent roles like actors in use-case diagrams ("in UML actors in use case diagrams represent a kind of subject..." [14]). Subjects typically perform their actions on objects in parallel and synchronize their activities via message exchange. According to Buchwald [5], the S-BPM notation should be a) closely aligned with existing standard notations (e.g., a subset of BPMN), b) as simple as possible, and c) readable and usable for business people so that they easily understand and modify models to take responsibility for defining their own processes [14].

The S-BPM modeling language is rooted in basic sentences in natural language, but also in the object-oriented paradigm and process algebras to allow for executable models [14]. The notation has only five modeling elements, the main elements *subject* and *message*, and additionally, three different state symbols (*send* state, *receive* state, and *function* state). The first two states describe the exchange of messages between subjects (subject X sends/receives message Y to/from subject Z), the third state refers to internal actions of subjects resulting in the acceptance or rejection of sent requests (subject X executes operation Y on object Z).

S-BPM modelling starts with the specifications of a communication diagram which defines the relevant subjects, the message they exchange and the involved business objects. The example diagram in Fig. 4 specifies the process of managing vacation requests. An employee sends a request to a manager (via the business object Vacation Request). The manager decides about the request. If it is approved then human resources

(HR) and the employee are informed accordingly. Otherwise, the employee gets a denial message.

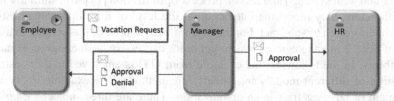

Fig. 4. Example of a S-BPM communication diagram.

Communication diagrams give an overview of projects, but details such as temporal relations and constraints between messages have to be specified in behavioral diagrams consisting of states, transitions, and messages. For example, the behavior of the subject Employee in Fig. 4 is described in the behavioral diagram shown in Fig. 5.

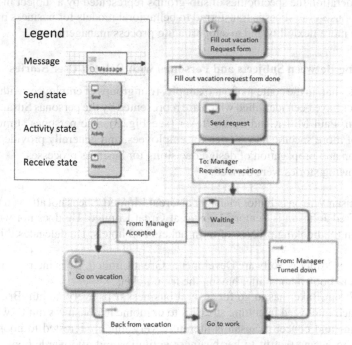

Fig. 5. Behavioral diagram for subject Employee.

According to this behavioral model, an employee first has to fill a form and then sent it to the manager. Afterwards, (s)he has to wait until a message from the manager arrives. If the request is accepted, (s)he can go on vacation and afterwards come back to work or (s)he has to go to work immediately. As to be seen, both communication diagrams and behavioral diagrams use a small set of modeling elements and have a simple structure.

3 Towards More Expressive Business-Process Models

Models in BPM 2.0 such as S-BPM put more emphasis on human interaction (with each other and with systems) and less on process optimization [14]. But similarly to use cases with actors, they model the interaction at the level of roles in an organizational setting which is often too abstract. For this reason, we propose in this section to use the models of Sect. 2 in an integrated way to get more expressive business-process models and flexibility. In the following, the example from [17] is employed to demonstrate a combination of different models and underlying methods. The example is about the management of business trips in an organization. There are three subjects: *Employee*, *Manager*, and *Agent*. The employee has to send a request for a business trip to the manager. An agent is available to support the booking of tickets and hotels. However, employees can also book hotels and tickets themselves according to preferences that are difficult to express to an agent. In particular, three aspects are considered:

• Subjects in S-BPM are refined by personas with their specific user stories.
• These stories are used to develop more differentiated behavioral models which take into consideration the specificities of sub-groups represented by a subject in S-BPM.
• The idea of use-case slices is transferred to behavioral models for business processes to achieve more flexibility and to support agile process management.

3.1 Mapping Between Subjects and Personas with Related User Stories

Let us assume that, in the context of our example, four groups of employees with specific characteristics have been identified which are represented by the personas Susan Wilson, Fred Johnson, Paul Miller, and Susan Baker (see Fig. 3). The personas stimulate the generation of more specific user stories for employees, and generally provide a source for inspiration and propagation of design decisions for business processes.

The following stories were derived:

• *Story 1:* Susan Wilson is Junior Manager at Great Limited. She is not allowed to travel.
• *Story 2:* Fred Johnson is Senior Manager at Great Limited. He does not want to be involved in the booking process of train tickets and hotels. He delegates this task to an agent.
• *Story 3:* Paul Miller is Software Developer at Great Limited. He is interested in trains and wants to book a hotel after having the train tickets.
• *Story 4:* Susan Baker has to go for several business trips every month. Because she is very much interested in culture she tries to combine her business duties with visits to museums and concerts. Susan is therefore very much interested to book a hotel according to events that fit to her business activities and afterwards book the train tickets.

In [11], we suggest to enhance use-case diagrams by persona information. However, stories can be used in a similar way. Figure 6 depicts a use case diagram, enhanced by persona-related stories. Both use case diagrams (sub-Sect. 2.2) and communication diagrams (sub-Sect. 2.4) provide an overview and can easily be 'decorated' by information about mappings between actors/subjects and personas and related stories.

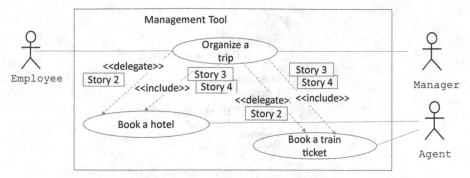

Fig. 6. Use-case diagram of Fig. 2, enriched by stories.

3.2 Behavioral Models with Slices

Actors in use case modeling and subjects, pools or lanes in business process modelling represent roles. However, not all 'instances' of an actor or subject behave in the same way. We have shown in previous work about use cases [11] how personas and their specific needs and task structures can help to develop a more differentiated view on actors. An actor can be represented by several personas. The resulting textual use case specifications show similarities and differences in the personas' interaction with the system.

Similarly, behavioral aspects of subjects, pools or lanes can be specified in more detail by taking into consideration the variations of related personas and user stories. Figure 7 shows a behavioral diagram which covers the above four different stories for subject *Employee* in our example.

Additionally, behavioral specifications should be sliced as use cases are sliced in [22] to support an agile development of models. In the example model in Fig. 7, two slices are specified that consist of two stories each. In this way, the model becomes more expressive and flexible but is still easy to read and modify by the stakeholders.

The combined use of personas, different types of stories, and sliced behavioral specifications also support the traceability of process models by documenting the reasons for their development.

The idea of sub-roles related to personas can also be applied to BPMN [4]. Figure 8 sketches a pool for an employee with the four different identified stories. We visualize the four stories by two different kind of lines that represent the two slices. Alternatively, stories could be linked to conditions at branches or as notes attached to the flow elements. Readability is improved in the same way as for S-BPM. Analysts might be inspired to identify other relevant stories which should be covered in the process model as well.

3.3 Discussion

The suggested transfer of ideas on model integration from user-centered design and agile software development to business process modeling seems to be justified for several reasons.

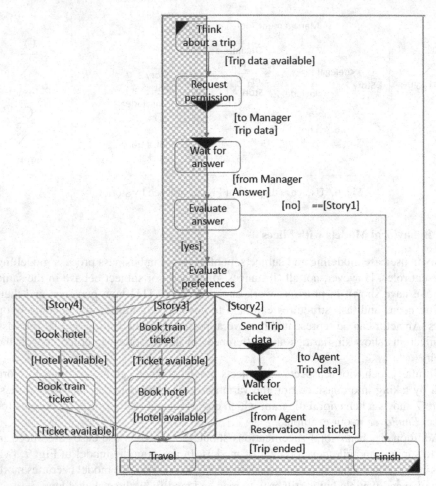

Fig. 7. Behavioral model for *Employee* with four stories, organized in two slices.

First, business-process models such as those in S-BPM take the acting elements (subjects) as starting point which represent, like actors in use case models, roles in an organization. Similar ideas are applicable to BPMN. Miller and Williams [26] comment with respect to the integration of the persona perspective to use cases that it allows: "to examine the different types of people who could play a role". A persona can be considered as a sub-classification of an actor. This applies to roles in other specifications as well. Randolph [29] mentions that personas better aid the designing of interaction with a system that meets a user's needs and goals, and use cases give more details about the specifics of users' task requirements. An integration of personas and business-process models can be similarly valuable to achieve more expressive models.

Second, personas are typically used for developing scenarios or stories at different levels of abstraction. This fits well with the idea of storytelling in business administration. Fog et al. [16] state: "Storytelling works as a supplement to traditional management tools.

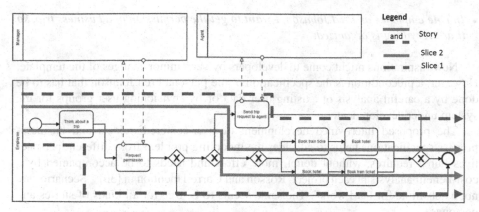

Fig. 8. Simplified BPMN-Diagram with four stories and two slices

For managers, the task is to use storytelling to anchor the company's values, visions, and culture within the organization."

Ciriello et al. [7] support this: "Our data shows that storytelling should not be reduced to the sole function of creating a common understanding between developers and users, but should also be seen as complementary practice, at eye level with prototyping, that can be an important means to support decision-making, transfer implicit knowledge, and facilitate communication, requirements elicitation and validation, as well as idea exploration and experimentation."

However, stories only provide these benefits if they are specified at different levels of abstraction. We distinguish the discussed stories in four levels:

1. Stories (sequences of actions) in Use Case 2.0 or in process models (e.g., Fig. 7 and Fig. 8),
2. Stories for personas (*e.g., Paul Miller is Software Developer at Great Limited. He is interested in trains and wants to book a hotel after having the train tickets.*),
3. User stories in agile development (e.g., *As an employee, I want to upload messages so that I can share them with others.*).
4. Current and envisaged stories as, for example, in [30].

Stories at lower levels of abstraction need to be grounded in stories at higher levels of abstraction which typically encourage more discussion and reasoning among stakeholders.

For user stories in agile development we would suggest an extended template that supports the combined use of roles and personas. It could look like:

- ***In role** <role> [as <persona>], **I want** <feature>, **so that** <reason>.*

In case that there are no sub-groups of personas the corresponding as-part can be omitted (optional part). An example can be the following story:

• *In role* employee *as* Fred Johnson, *I want to* get the permission of a business trip, *so that* everything is organized.

New inspirations might come to developers by such minor changes of the template. However, a precondition is the specification of the persona Fred Johnson that has to be done by a careful analysis of existing user data or by envisioning user groups for the system under development.

The proposed intertwined development of user-centered models and business-process specifications helps to consider the modeling problem from different perspectives but it requires, without doubt, more effort and needs to be accompanied by a cost-benefit analysis in each project. Rosson and Carroll mention in [30]: "Scenarios are not a substitute for hard work". The same seems to be true for all kinds of stories and personas.

4 Summary and Outlook

Stakeholders engage better with personas and stories than with abstract descriptions of user groups, tasks and processes. This paper discusses the cross-pollination of stories, use cases, personas and business-process models. We identify four levels of abstraction for stories and show how the different stories and concepts from agile software development such as use case slices can be used to develop more expressive and flexible business-process models. Examples in S-BPM and BPMN are provided.

Future work includes the development of methodological and tool support for the suggested intertwined development of the different models.

A systematic development of stories at different levels of abstraction can facilitate the application of techniques such as story splitting and slicing and supports an agile development of process models. Further case studies should provide rules for this approach.

References

1. Acuña, S.T., Castro, J.W., Juzgado, N.J.: A HCI technique for improving requirements elicitation. Inf. Softw. Technol. **54**(12), 1357–1375 (2012)
2. Bittner, K., Spence, I.: Use Case Modeling. Addison-Wesley, Boston (2002)
3. Blomquist, A., Arvola, M.: Personas in action: ethnography in an interaction design team. In: Proceedings of NordiCHI 2002, pp. 197–200. ACM (2002)
4. BPMN: Business Process Model and Notation (2011). https://www.bpmn.org/. Accessed 16 Feb 2022
5. Buchwald, H.: Potential building blocks of S-BPM. In: Buchwald, H., Fleischmann, A., Seese, D., Stary, C. (eds.) S-BPM ONE 2009. CCIS, vol. 85, pp. 123–135. Springer, Heidelberg (2010). https://doi.org/10.1007/978-3-642-15915-2_10
6. Chapman, C.N., Milham, R.P.: The personas' new clothes: methodological and practical arguments against a popular method. In: The Human Factors and Ergonomics Society Annual Meeting, pp. 634–636 (2006)

7. Ciriello, R.F., Richter, A., Schwabe, G.: When prototyping meets storytelling: practices and malpractices in innovating software firms. In: Proceedings of the 39th International Conference on Software Engineering: Software Engineering in Practice Track (ICSE-SEIP 2017), pp. 163–172. IEEE Press (2017)
8. Cockburn, A.: Writing Effective Use Cases. Addison-Wesley, Boston (2000)
9. Cooper, A.: The Inmates Are Running the Asylum. Macmillan Publishing Co., Inc, New York (1999)
10. Denning, S.: The Leader's Guide to Storytelling: Mastering the Art and Discipline of Business Narrative, Jossey-Bass a Wiley Imprint (2011)
11. Dittmar, A., Forbrig, P.: Integrating personas and use case models. In: Lamas, D., Loizides, F., Nacke, L., Petrie, H., Winckler, M., Zaphiris, P. (eds.) INTERACT 2019. LNCS, vol. 11746, pp. 666–686. Springer, Cham (2019). https://doi.org/10.1007/978-3-030-29381-9_40
12. Eriksson, E., Artman, H., Swartling A.: The secret life of a persona: when the personal becomes private. In: Proceedings of CHI 2013, pp. 2677–2686. ACM (2013)
13. Faily, S.: Bridging User-centered design and requirements engineering with GRL and persona cases. In: de Castro, J.B., Franch, X., Mylopoulos, J., Yu, E.S.K. (eds.) Proceedings of the 5th International i* Workshop 2011 (CEUR Workshop Proceedings), vol. 766, pp. 114–119. CEUR-WS.org (2011)
14. Fleischmann, A.: What is S-BPM? In: Buchwald, H., Fleischmann, A., Seese, D., Stary, C. (eds.) S-BPM ONE 2009. CCIS, vol. 85, pp. 85–106. Springer, Heidelberg (2010). https://doi.org/10.1007/978-3-642-15915-2_7
15. Fleischmann, A., Kannengiesser, U., Schmidt, W., Stary, C.: Subject-oriented modeling and execution of multiagent business processes. In: 2013 IEEE/WIC/ACM International Conferences on Intelligent Agent Technology, IAT 2013, 17–20 November 2013, Atlanta, Georgia, USA, pp. 138–145 (2013). https://doi.org/10.1109/WI-IAT.2013.102
16. Fog, K., Budtz, C., Munch, P., Blanchette, S.: Storytelling as a management tool. In: Fog, K., Budtz, C., Munch, P., Blanchette, S. (eds.) Storytelling: Branding in Practice. Springer, Heidelberg (2010). https://doi.org/10.1007/978-3-540-88349-4_6
17. Forbrig, P., Dittmar, A.: Applying agile methods and personas to S-BPM. In: Proceedings of the S-BPM ONE Conference, Seville, Spain, pp. 8:1–8:10 (2019)
18. Di Francescomarino, C., et al.: A bit of "Persona", a bit of "Goal", a bit of "Process" ... a recipe for analyzing user intensive software systems. In: iStar (CEUR Workshop Proceedings), vol. 586, pp. 36–40. CEUR-WS.org (2010)
19. Grudin, J., Pruitt, J.: Personas, participatory design and product development: an infrastructure for engagement. In: Proceedings of PDC 2002, pp. 144–161 (2002)
20. Jacobson, I., Christerson, M., Jonsson, P., Övergaard, G.: Object-Oriented Software Engineering: A Use Case Driven Approach. Addison-Wesley, Boston (1992)
21. Jacobson, I., Spence, I., Bittner, K.: The Guide to Succeeding with Use Cases (2011). https://www.ivarjacobson.com/sites/default/files/field_iji_file/article/use-case_2_0_j an11.pdf. Accessed 14 Feb 2022
22. Jacobson, I., Spence, I., Kerr, B.: Use-case 2.0. Commun. ACM 59(5), 61–69 (2016)
23. Jones, M.C., Floyd, I.R., Twidale, M.B.: Teaching design with personas. In: Proceedings of HCIEd (2008)
24. Lawrence, R., Green, P.: The Humanizing Work Guide to Splitting User Stories (2020). https://www.humanizingwork.com/the-humanizing-work-guide-to-splitting-user-stories/. Accessed 14 Feb 2022
25. Li, M.: How to Use Storytelling as Management Tool, The Ohio State University, Fisher Collage of Business (2020). https://fisher.osu.edu/blogs/leadreadtoday/how-use-storytelling-management-tool. Accessed 27 Apr 2022
26. Miller, G., Williams, L.: Personas: moving beyond role-based requirements engineering. Technical report, North Carolina State University, Department of Computer Science (2006)

27. Nielsen, L.: Personas. In: The Encyclopedia of Human-Computer Interaction, 2nd edn (2013)
28. Quesenbery, W., Brooks, K.: Storytelling for User Experience: Crafting Stories for Better Design. Rosenfeld Media (2010)
29. Randolph, G.: Use-cases and personas: a case study in light-weight user interaction design for small development projects. Inf. Sci. Int. J. Emerg. Transdisc. **7**, 105–116 (2004)
30. Rosson, M.B., Carroll, J.M.: The human-computer interaction handbook: fundamentals, evolving technologies and emerging applications, pp. 1032–1050. L. Erlbaum Associates Inc., Hillsdale. Chapter Scenario-Based Design (2003). http://dl.acm.org/citation.cfm?id= 772072.772137
31. Schneidewind, L., Hörold, S., Mayas, C., Krömker, H., Falke, S., Pucklitsch, T.: How personas support requirements engineering. In: Proceedings of the First International Workshop on Usability and Accessibility Focused Requirements Engineering (UsARE 2012), pp. 1–5. IEEE (2012)
32. Thier, K.: Storytelling mit der 3-Akt-Struktur: Wie Sie mit der 3-Akt-Struktur authentische Geschichten erzählen und Kunden sowie Mitarbeiter binden - der Leitfaden (Quick Guide). Springer Verlag (2017)

Proposal for Determining the Angular Position of Artificial Intraocular Lens in the Human Eye

Martin Fus[1]([✉]) [iD], Josef Pavlicek[2] [iD], Sarka Pitrova[1] [iD], and Michal Hruska[2] [iD]

[1] Faculty of Biomedical Engineering, Czech Technical University in Prague, Prague, Czech Republic
martin.fus@cvut.cz

[2] Faculty of Engineering, Czech University of Life Sciences in Prague, Prague, Czech Republic

Abstract. Any clouding of the lens of the eye causing distortion of its transparency and scattering of transmitted light is called a cataract. The solution to this pathological condition affecting the quality of life is phacoemulsification of the cloudy contents of the human lens and its replacement with an artificial intraocular lens (IOL). The surgeon has the opportunity to influence the refractive state of the eye for optimal postoperative visual acuity by choosing an appropriate IOL. In addition, a certain group of patients has an ametropia called corneal astigmatism, which needs to be corrected with a so-called toric IOL, in which the key criterion for the success of the correction is its angular position in the capsular bag. Deviation from the intended angular position of the implanted lens can lead to refractive surprise, i.e. the patient's postoperative visual acuity does not reach 100% of its own potential. In clinical practice, however, there is no conventional technique or tool for retrospectively determining the postoperative angular position to the required 1° accuracy. Thus, the intent of this paper was to create a custom design for automating IOL detection using postoperative patient images from the Verion reference unit and a specific lens model, the SN6ATx. The problem addressed is the automation of finding the optical part of the intraocular artificial lens using machine vision technologies based on convolutional operations on the image. The study presents the actual approach and methodology of the self-developed solution.

Keywords: Cataract surgery · Artificial toric intraocular lens · Astigmatism · Computer vison · Artificial intelligence · Convolution methods · Histogram · Sobel filters · Erosion

1 Introduction

Image recognition analysis and technology can already be considered a multidisciplinary field due to its wide range of applications. The development of segmentation methods, automatic multilevel thresholding, image registration, key features or edge detection in a wide range of medical imaging technologies is constantly pushing the possibilities of

---

The original version of this chapter was revised: The affiliation of the author Michal Hruska has been corrected. The correction to this chapter is available at
https://doi.org/10.1007/978-3-031-17728-6_12

E. Babkin et al. (Eds.): MOBA 2022, LNBIP 457, pp. 19–26, 2022.
https://doi.org/10.1007/978-3-031-17728-6_2

diagnosing pathological conditions. Semantics can be considered as the biggest obstacle for image analysis in clinical medicine, which fails due to too much visual variability in clinical findings. However, the application of artificial intelligence, neural networks or self-learning algorithms provides the potential for greater success in object recognition and classification even in more complex clinical images [1].

Within the field of ophthalmology, these methods are useful tools in clinical practice, for example, for automatic assessment of the thickness of the neuroretinal nerve fiber layer from retinal images obtained by optical coherence tomography, analysis of images reflected by the cornea for corneal keratometry or topography, or the use of the so-called "image-guided navigation system" during surgery. In cataract surgery, where an intraocular lens (IOL) is implanted after phacoemulsification of the opacified lens itself, the assistance of these systems allows the surgeon to control in real time the position and angle of the intraocular lens with an accuracy of one angular degree in specific cases of corneal astigmatism correction [2].

For the diagnosis of patients after cataract surgery, which could help the ophthalmologist to assess the position of the intraocular lens in the eye, the potential of image analysis in clinical practice is practically unused. In cataract surgery, in addition to removing the cloudy lens itself, the surgeon also has the option of implanting an artificial lens with individual parameters that will allow the patient to have excellent distance visual acuity without the need for spectacle correction. In cases where additional correction of corneal astigmatism is required, the implantation of a so-called toric intraocular lens is necessary for this purpose. When evaluating the success of the resulting postoperative visual acuity, the position of the IOL in the capsular bag such as decentration, tilt, axial position and angular orientation of the toric IOL become crucial parameters. Custom proposal of software solution for the universal objective evaluation of factors influencing intraocular correction of astigmatism was developed and successfully used in clinical practice [3, 4].

However, the most critical of the positional factors mentioned above in relation to astigmatism correction is the angular position of the toric IOL. Simulations demonstrate that misalignment is not linearly related to loss of visual fidelity, but $5°$ of misalignment causes a loss of 7.03%, and misalignment of $10°$ causes to 11.9% of loss of visual fi-delivery of image quality [5]. Therefore, this study focuses on that particular factor. The main aim of the study is to present our own proposal of the possibility to automate the evaluation of the angular position of a specific model of the toric intraocular lens on a specific output image from the reference unit of the navigation system, where the semi-position of the SN6ATx lens will be approximated based on the haptic position of the IOL.

2 Materials and Methods

The studied problem is the automation of finding the optical part of the intraocular artificial lens on real test images of operated patients. The input for the task is a digital photograph of the patient's eye acquired in infrared mode using the reference unit of the Verion navigation system (Fig. 1). The desired result is the automated finding of its optical part and subsequently its angular orientation. Knowing the constant lens design, the orientation of the correction axis can be determined indirectly by identifying the position of the stabilizing mechanism, so called haptics (Fig. 2).

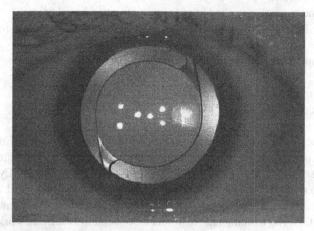

Fig. 1. Example of an input image of a toric IOL whose contours are highlighted by infrared light reflected from the retina.

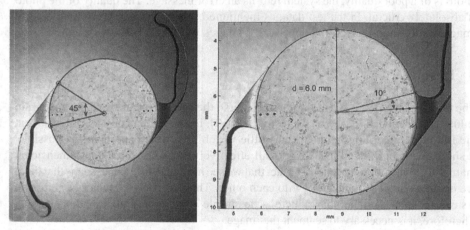

Fig. 2. Graphical verification of the position of the marker points of angular orientation relative to the toric IOL haptics [6].

Because there are a limited number of photos of artificial lenses (tens of pieces) it is not possible to use AI technology. Common and applicable for this task deep learning neural networks like YOLO 5 [7, 8] require at least 2000 images for basic training for a similar task. However, 10–100 thousand images in the training set are generally recommended. Each such image has to be correctly labelled, which again introduces a large amount of labor. A not insignificant problem is the relatively low quality of the images obtained for the experiment (230 KB in png format). For machine vision tasks, the more "high-quality" the image is, i.e., it contains more image data (pixels), the wider range of image recognition methods can be used [9].

For the above reasons, it was decided to proceed in a hybrid way:

a) Input image control,
b) balancing and normalizing the photo using histogram-based filters,
c) segmenting the image by erosion and joining the remaining objects using geometric shapes,
d) Inserting approximation circles bounding the edges of the lens using an iterative method,
e) by iterative method we find the haptics, its orientation
f) finding the decentralization of the lens.

C# was chosen as the appropriate programming language for the task. Current frameworks for image operations are available for it. In the field of artificial intelligence, Python is the primary language today. However, learned models that would use Python almost always contain a wrapper for calls from other languages. If this is not possible, then there is a way to reprogram a favoured neural network (which will be experimentally verified in Python) into C#. The C# language also has a convenient.Net framework that allows full windowing. The application is experimental, its suitable architecture is the so-called Fat Client. The captured photo is read by the system and displayed for analysis. If the photo is of a poor quality, the system returns an error message. The quality of the photo is absolutely crucial. In the test data, as mentioned, we do not have very high-quality images. Only anon-imaged and downscaled images from the VERION system.

3 Results

The read image is processed in several steps. First, the photo is cleaned and the histogram values are calculated. Based on the histogram [10], image normalization is done so that the following algorithms work with as little variability of the data inputs as possible. It should be kept in mind that we are still effectively working with a two-dimensional matrix of atomic points (pixels). The fact that we see a circle in the image means that there are distinct points that are adjacent to each other. The lens is not circular but elliptical. As can be seen from the image, there is no simple circle to be found mathematically. Therefore, it is necessary to segment the image.

The cleaned and normalized image is first stripped of the central part and the surroundings using knowledge of the problem (solution context). This significantly narrows the area of points we work with. Next, the center of the image is found, which is important for future object retrieval, the histogram is calculated again and the image is converted to binary form. Based on the normalized values, a morphological operation is first performed to erode the image, thus removing unnecessary points (noise objects, see Minor points in the image) from the image and making the main contours of the objects visible (Fig. 3). Using a convolution kernel shifted first along the X-axis and then along the Y-axis, we suppress the minor points and highlight the major points. The result is the point map that we will work with next [11].

Now we work with blocks of points - blobs [12]. Using iterative methods, we perform the following steps:

Fig. 3. Pre-prepared IOL image before segmentation.

a) Draw a circle in the spiral from the center clockwise.
b) Count the points through which the circle passes and add the adjacent points, the adjacency of the points is determined by the setup, but it turns out that it is useful to have ± 2 pixels from the edge in this problem (this is very important to find the shape of the lens, which can be elliptical due to its potential tilt.
c) Get all possible existing circles from the center of the image.
d) From those, again using an iterative method, select those whose radius logically corresponds to the possible sizes of the lens and at the same time pass through the largest number of points. These are the boundary points of the image and are presumably the inner and outer edges of the lens. For-since the lens is elliptical, let us now consider the circle as a thick circle, or rather the area not containing the greatest number of points statistically. This is then the favored result.
e) Now the found circles are transferred back to the image (we are no longer working with a binary image) and highlight the circles (Figs. 4 and 5).
f) Using the iterative method, the line is moved along the favourite circle so that it passes through as many points with haptics, as possible. In this way, we find the angle of haptics of the lens.

It would, of course, be possible and probably necessary in the future (unless replacing this algorithm with a suitable neural network) to rotate the ellipse. This is, of course, computationally much more complicated, so for now we have used the circle that best passes through the largest number of points for the approximation, and with it we get the X, Y coordinates of its center. Since Cartesian space is considered, it is easy to find their distance using a known Eq. (1):

$$|AB| = \sqrt{(b_1 - a_1)^2 + (b_2 - a_2)^2} \tag{1}$$

where $|AB|$ is resulted distance of decentration in absolute value, a_1 and b_1 are X coordinates and a_2 and b_2 are Y coordinates of first and second point.

Fig. 4. Demonstration of finding the center and outline of the optical part of the IOL.

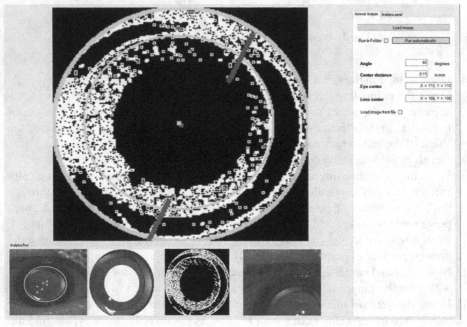

Fig. 5. Demonstration of finding the center and contour of an optical part including an approximation of the IOL haptics.

The results of the solution are currently applicable almost exclusively to the highest quality images with the best contrast. The algorithm fails significantly if the lens is significantly elliptical (caused by IOL tilt in the frontal plane). We are aware of this problem. It is solvable by iterating through the ellipse to the location of the chosen lens. Another limiting factor is the quality of the images. If the lighting conditions are poor and the contrast of the lens relative to the surroundings is low, the method of eroding and back-connecting the remaining points into blobs fails. On suitable high contrast images, the system is functional. The method is therefore applicable.

4 Discussion

In the clinical ophthalmology praxis, several proposals can be found of software and graphic solutions for determining the postoperative angular position of the toric IOL. A popular universal tool is the *Goniotrans* application, which projects a transparent angular scale onto the underlying image that can be freely modified by the user [13]. Another alternative free of cost are software that allows the manual creation of a graphical line with the output of the angular value relative to the horizontal, one example is Angle Meter for smartphone use or software in our previous published study [3, 14]. Another approach is to use the functionality of a commonly used graphical editor with slight modifications, i.e., interleaving transparent scales and templates [15, 16]. However, all these approaches depend on subjective and manual evaluation by the user, which can be misleading and time-consuming. Therefore, our approach was guided by the path of automating the respective objectification of the evaluation.

As this is an experimental method, we cannot yet speak of comparing the results with a quantifiable test set. On images meeting suitable sub-conditions it works at 90%. It is possible to work towards the ideal condition using more sophisticated filters. A major and debatable issue is the unsuitability of the algorithm for lower quality images. And this "lower" quality is still bridge able for humans without much difficulty. A human being can find the artificial lens in the image even if our algorithm fails. The question is why. There are several answers. The human brain and the human eye are significantly more sophisticated systems than our computer algorithm and are equipped to recognize shapes, complete with possible patterns (see hallucinations and perceptual illusions). This allows humans to approximate and fill in missing information in an image, such as the blind spot.

It is possible that even more sophisticated filters and methods of working with the image to be found. We can define a whole range of them. Starting from the mentioned approximation of the lens by post-motion ellipse to interlacing several images on top of each other with a slight shift of XY coordinates. This simulates bifocal vision and highlights edges in the image. Another option is to introduce suitable artificial intelligence technologies such as YOLOv5 [7, 8].

5 Conclusion

The next step of our work is a quantifiable comparison of our automated method with a human specialist. We will publish further on this in future peri-analyses. We will now venture to say that if we have images of significantly higher quality, and not just screenshots of the Verion system, our solution will be able to replace a human operator at least in those cases where images are appropriate. This will reduce the burden on the working specialist and achieve the necessary level of objectification of the evaluation of the lens angular position factor and its decentration.

The idea stated at the beginning of this paper is still valid, the machine is able to see what a human sees. However, we are still limited by the computational capacity of computers, their speed and, last but not least, the development of suitable algorithms (after all, nature did not create man overnight). However, the current era of deep neural networks allowing to learn the presented patterns (although still requiring a huge amount of learning sets) and convolutional operations with images now perfectly elaborated are the tools with which we will be able to solve the mentioned task in the future (and we believe very soon).

References

1. Szeliski, R.: Computer Vision. Springer, London (2011). https://doi.org/10.1007/978-1-84882-935-0. ISBN 978-1-84882-934-3
2. Grytz, R.: Computational modeling and remodeling of human eye tissues as biomechanical structures at multiple scales. Aachen Shaker (2009). ISBN 9783832279585
3. Fus, M., Pitrova, S.: Evaluation of decentration, tilt and angular orientation of toric intraocular lens. Clin. Ophthalmol. **15**, 4755–4761 (2021). https://doi.org/10.2147/OPTH.S346968. PMID: 34983999; PMCID: PMC8699775
4. Fus, M., Pitrova, S., Maresova, K., Lestak, J.: Changes of intraocular lens position induced by Nd: YAG capsulotomy. Biomed Pap Med Fac Univ Palacky Olomouc Czech Repub (2021). https://doi.org/10.5507/bp.2021.014. Epub ahead of print. PMID: 33724262
5. Tognetto, D., et al.: Quality of images with toric intraocular lenses. J. Cataract Refract. Surg. **44**(3), 376–381 (2018). https://doi.org/10.1016/j.jcrs.2017.10.053. PMID: 29703290
6. Fus, M.: Determining angular position of toric intraocular lens [Diploma thesis]. FBME, Czech Technical University in Prague
7. Liu, T., Zhou, B., Zhao, Y., Yan, S.: Ship detection algorithm based on improved YOLO V5. In: 2021 6th International Conference on Automation, Control and Robotics Engineering (CACRE), July 2016
8. Hamplová, A., Pavlíček, J.: Object recognition tool for "smart nest boxes". In: Proceedings of IAC in Budapest (2020)
9. Pavlíček, J., et al.: Automated wildlife recognition. AGRIS on-line Pap. Econ. Inform. **10**(1), 51–60 (2018). https://doi.org/10.7160/aol.2018.100105. ISSN 1804-1930
10. Scott, D.W.: Averaged shifted histogram. Wiley Interdiscip. Rev. Comput. Stat. **2**(2), 160–164 (2009). https://doi.org/10.1002/wics.54
11. Sobel, I.: History and Definition of the Sobel Operator (2014). https://www.researchgate.net/publication/239398674_An_Isotropic_3x3_Image_Gradient_Operator
12. Lindeberg, T.: Detection salient blob-like image structure and their scales with a scale-space primal sketch: a method for focus-of-attention. Int. J. Comput. Vis. **11**(3), 283–318 (1993). https://doi.org/10.1007/BF01469346. S2CID 11998035
13. Goniotrans: A Simple Tool to Refer Angles. Eventos Médicos y Sociales, S.L. Home User manual License Contact (2012). http://www.goniotrans.com/. Accessed 18 Mar 2017
14. Teichman, J.C.: Simple technique to measure toric intraocular lens alignment and stability using a smartphone. J. Cataract Refract. Surg. (JCRS) **40**(12), 1949–1952 (2014). https://doi.org/10.1016/j.jcrs.2014.09.029
15. Shah, G.D., et al.: Software-based assessment of postoperative rotation of toric intraocular lens. J Cataract Refract. Surg. **35**(3), 413–418 (2009). https://doi.org/10.1016/j.jcrs.2008.10.057. PMID: 19251130
16. Becker, K.A., Auffarth, G.U., Völcker, H.E.: Messmethode zur Bestimmung der Rotation und der Dezentrierung von Intraokularlinsen [Measurement method for the determination of rotation and decentration of intraocular lenses]. Ophthalmologe **101**(6), 600–603 (2004). https://doi.org/10.1007/s00347-003-0951-7. PMID 15197576

Agile Game in Practice

Ondřej Havazík[1], Petra Pavlíčková[2(✉)], and Jan Rydval[3]

[1] Faculty of Economics and Management, Czech University of Life Sciences Prague,
Kamýcká 129, 165 00 Prague – Suchdol, Czech Republic
`havazik@pef.czu.cz`
[2] Faculty of Information Technology, Czech Technical University in Prague, Thákurova 9,
160 00 Prague 6, Czech Republic
`petra.pavlickova@fit.cvut.cz`
[3] Faculty of Economics and Management, Czech University of Life Sciences Prague,
Kamýcká 129, 165 00 Prague – Suchdol, Czech Republic
`rydval@pef.czu.cz`

Abstract. This paper aims to assess the suitability of the two teaching approaches to practice the agile Scrum methodology. The first approach uses a desk game to teach agile methodology, and the second approach uses an agile game with Jira software. The participants of these games evaluate both methods from the point of view of their satisfaction and usefulness. The participants like the use of Jira software, which is now widely used for IT project management in real practice. Introduced agile games increase students' ability to appropriately communicate and to work together like a team, which are basic principles of agile methodologies. Teaching agile methodology through games is very beneficial and positively evaluated among participants. Therefore, the presented games can be considered useful for learning the basic principles of agile project management.

Keywords: Agile · Agile game · Jira software · Scrum · Team roles

1 Introduction

Agile approaches have recently been gradually applied in many companies involved not only in software development. These approaches are used in small and medium-sized companies and large corporations. Agile methods consider the fact that software development projects are mostly too complex to define their full scope at the phase of project planning. The requirements of these projects cannot be fully specified in ad-vance because they are rarely fully defined at the beginning of the project [2, 3]. Agile methods also encourage: close collaboration between the development team and the customer, adapting to change, and working in rapid, iterative development cycles. This all distinguishes them from traditional project management methods (waterfall approach).

However, despite the numerous successes of introducing agile methodologies into how projects are managed, most organizations struggle to fully implement agile methodologies into project management [12]. Although agile methods are claimed to be easy to

E. Babkin et al. (Eds.): MOBA 2022, LNBIP 457, pp. 27–40, 2022.
https://doi.org/10.1007/978-3-031-17728-6_3

understand [9, 13], they are difficult to follow in practice. One of the reasons for the lack of adherence to the basic principles of agile methodologies is that university graduates (mostly the future members of project teams) are not prepared to manage and be managed [11]. These are two essential skills of project team members that a successful team cannot cooperate without if any agile methodology is used. Scrum methodology is in Pinto's opinion [11], one of the most suitable agile methodologies for team and project management. Schwaber and Sutherland [14] describe Scrum as simple to understand but relatively difficult to master. Therefore, it is necessary to appropriately support the teaching of agile approaches, both in companies and in universities with project management students.

Supporting the teaching of agile approaches in universities is not easy [1]. When teaching agile methodologies, such as agile software development, it is crucial to consider the following factors: student collaboration in teams, communication with the customer, and well-defined project scope. Kropp and Meier [7], based on their experiments with teaching agile methodologies, found that using agile methodologies in teaching has a positive impact on student learning out-comes. Yilmaz and O'Connor [16] also demonstrated a positive effect on job performance by using agile methodologies teaching with the help of gamification for software developers. Thus, it is clear that teaching and practicing agile methodologies improve teamwork and effectiveness. However, the question remains, what form and way to choose for teaching agile methodologies.

It can be difficult to motivate software developers to use agile tools because they often claim that agile tools disrupt their workflows. Therefore, Yilmaz and O'Connor [16] introduced gamification of different parts of the Scrum methodology to improve its adoption. Their gamification consisted, for instance, of incorporating some sprint log's items into a points system so that only team members with a sufficient number of accumulated points could participate on such sprint log's items. Points were then collected for completing individual tasks using Scrum tools. Yilmaz and O'Connor [16] thus represent the use of gamification to encourage software developers to use the tools of the agile methodology with the necessary regularity. Another way to teach agile methodologies is through agile gamification using virtual reality. Mayor and López-Fernández [10] present virtual reality technologies as an appropriate medium for active, effective, and innovative teaching of agile methodologies. However, it is not necessary to always use highly sophisticated tools to teach agile methodologies. Kurkovsky [8] designed a relatively simple Lego game to introduce the basic concepts and principles of the Scrum methodology. This game provides students with the opportunity to play different scrum roles and measure the work speed of the development team in two sprints (iterations).

The basic principles of the Scrum methodology without using highly sophisticated tools are also introduced by Havazík and Pavlíčková [4] through a desk game. In this game, students work together in a team where each student plays a specified role. Although the project splits into sprints and the tools of the Scrum methodology are used, there is no need to use any sophisticated software in this game. Such a game allows learning the basic principles of the agile methodology, but it does not allow trying out the different software used in a real agile environment. Therefore, Havazík and Pavlíčková [6] came up with an improvement of their agile game, which consists in using the Jira software. In this game, students work in an agile team using Jira software and learn the basics of its use and also the basics of the agile Scrum methodology. However, the question still remains which teaching methods are suitable for learning the basic principles of agile methodology or which learning method is perceived as suitable by the participants of agile games themselves.

This paper aims to assess the suitability of two teaching approaches to practice the agile Scrum methodology. The first approach uses a desk game to teach agile methodology, and the second approach uses an agile game with Jira software. The participants of these games evaluate both methods. Both in terms of their satisfaction with the game itself and the usefulness of both teaching approaches in learning the basic principles of the agile Scrum methodology.

This paper first briefly describes the basic principles of agile and introduces the agile Scrum methodology. Then the group of students who participated in the research is presented. The paper describes two ways of teaching the agile approach in IT project management (a desk game to teach the agile methodology and an agile game with Jira software). This is followed by the respondents' evaluation and assessment of both teaching methods, indicating which way students find more suitable for teaching and understanding the basic principles of agile approaches.

2   Materials and Methods

2.1   Agile Principles

The traditional way to build software, used by mall and large companies and corporations, was a sequential development life cycle known as "the waterfall." This approach has strengths and weaknesses. Its great strength is logical "think before you build", write it all down, follow a plan, and keep everything as organized as possible. It has just one great weakness: humans are involved [15].

Agile development methodologies were born out of the belief that the approach would be more grounded in the human and product development realities of learning, innovation and change, which in turn would deliver better results and happy customers. Agile principles put more emphasis on building functional software that people can use quickly versus spending a lot of time writing specifications up front. Agile development focuses on cross-functional teams that are empowered to make decisions versus large hierarchies and divisions by function. And it focuses on rapid iterations with constant customer input. When people hear about agile development or Scrum, they often get a flash of recognition - it sounds similar to the days of start-ups when "we'll just do it" was common.

2.2   Scrum

Scrum is an iterative, incremental approach to optimize predictability and to control and manage risk. The beauty of Srum is that it is domain and technology independent. Scrum is used in companies in various business areas and even in individual families when planning weddings, family chores and other smaller tasks. It is a significant innovation in the way to get things done faster and better while making the work more rewarding for everyone involved [14, 15].

2.3 Scrum Team

The fundamental unit of Scrum is a small team of people, a Scrum team. The Scrum team [14] consists of one Scrum Master, one Product Owner, and Developers. Within a Scrum team, there are no subteams or hierarchies. Scrum teams are cross-functional and self-managing. The Scrum team should be a small team, typically 10 or fewer people. If Scrum teams become too large, they should consider reorganizing into multiple Scrum teams, each focused on the same product. Therefore, they should share the same Product Goal, Product Backlog, and Product Owner.

The Scrum team is responsible for all product-related activities from stakeholder collaboration, verification, maintenance, operation, experimentation, research and development, and anything else that might be required. The entire Scrum Team is accountable for creating a valuable, useful increment every Sprint. Scrum defines three typical Scrum roles: the Developers, the Product Owner, and the Scrum Master.

Developers are the people in the scrum team who contribute to the development in each sprint.

The product owner is responsible for maximizing the value of the product that results from the work of the Scrum team.

The Scrum Master is responsible for the implementation of the Scrum Team. He does this by helping everyone understand the theory and practice of Scrum, both within the Scrum team and within the organization. The Scrum Master is responsible for the effectiveness of the Scrum team.

2.4 Group of Tested Students

For comparison, we have two very similar target groups of students. Both ways of teaching the agile approach in IT project management (a desk game to teach the agile methodology and an agile game with Jira software) took place with students of the Faculty of Economics and Management of the Czech University of Life Sciences Prague.

The students were from two groups, one could almost say identical, both in terms of their number, practice, and field of study. Let's start with the number of students and the focus because the two sections are almost identical. The game was played with students in the 2nd year of the follow-up master's degree of information technology in the subject IT project management. The first group (Group 1) with which the game was played in the autumn of 2019 had a total of 63 respondents. With the second group (Group 2), the game was played two years later, in the fall of 2021. In 2020, it was not played due to the covid-19 pandemic and online teaching. For these reasons, the game was also converted to an online version, found in an article from the MoBa 2021 conference [6]. In the second group of students, the number was very similar, namely 74 respondents. In the part where the two groups differ, however, is the form of play that the game was played with the students.

2.5 Description of Both Types of Games

In principle, this is a simple agile game based on a fictional project in the field of information technology (web and mobile application). There are two essential sides, namely the customer, represented by a teacher, and a supplier of a graphical solution, which consists of 4 to 6 students team. Students have to practice agile deliveries of individual solutions in a team; the roles in the group are also adapted to this. Roles with specific skillsets carry out graphic work, and management roles oversee project priorities and deadlines. More about the whole agile game can be read in the article from the ERIE conference from 2020 [4].

This paper describes the games as being played directly with the first (Group1), and the second group (Group2). The first game was more or less conceived as a desk game. The students did not use any professional IT software or tool. Everything was implemented using a whiteboard, cards, and presenting the solution to the customer in a personal form, including acceptance of the solution.

The second group has already played the game mainly in one of the most well-known development software, JIRA from Atlassian. All tasks were created in a specific project. The proposals were uploaded as an attachment. The solution was approved by the customer entirely (and exclusively) in the environment of the Jira tool. The implementation of the work remained classical in the form of graphic solutions on paper. Still, this will also be eliminated in the future, and game graphic designs will also be implemented in one of the online tools. How this type of game can be converted to JIRA software can be found in the article from the CoDit conference from 2020 [5].

The game had common features in several ways. For example, both groups of students had to carry out a risk analysis before the start of the game, which directly affected the course of the game and the restrictions that occurred during the sprints. Students draw a risk card at the beginning of each sprint. If they didn't prevent it properly, during the sprint, they face impacts such as the inability to work on undivided designs, communicate with the customer, etc. The demands on the completed work also do not differ. Students was forced to achieve the same quality of solutions in both types of games. They differ only in the transmission of results to the customer and their acceptance.

3   Results

First, students were asked if they had any real experience with agile project management and Scrum methodology, if they had at least heard of it but did not have real experience, or if they did not come into contact with it at all. The answers of the two interviewed groups did not differ dramatically; the deviation of the individual responses was a maximum of about 10%. In first section of the Table no.1 is possible to see a difference in knowledge of agile project management before the game. As can be seen, the complete practical ignorance of agile management was greater among students in 2021 (Group 2), but also knowledge. At the bottom was a light experience.

The second important question for better identification of students was whether they came into contact with the agile Scrum methodology in which the game is implemented. Second section of the table shows lack of knowledge of agile methods is dramatically more significant than the lack of knowledge of agile management as such in the case of both groups. Most students have never come into contact with the Scrum framework or have not used it in practice. Here the results differ minimally as you can see from Table 1 and 2 below.

Table 1. Knowledge of and agile approach

Agile approach knowledge	Group 1	%	Group 2	%
Have a real experience	17	27.0	21	28.4
A little	20	31.7	16	21.6
Not at all	26	41.3	37	50.0
Number of students	63	100	74	100

Table 2. Knowledge of a scrum framework

Scrum framework knowledge	Group 1	%	Group 2	%
Have a real experience	11	17.5	11	14.9
A little	13	20.6	11	14.9
Not at all	39	61.9	52	70.3
Number of students	63	100	74	100

An integral part and also a partial purpose of the game is for students to actively communicate with each other and practice teamwork, which takes place on projects and is one of the critical activities. Based on this, students were asked how satisfied they were with the communication in their team. Here you would expect that the results could differ depending on the style of play. According to Graph No. 4, it can be seen that in the version of the game, where students submitted assignments and had themselves accepted in the online JIRA environment, communication was generally at a better level than in the case of the group that played the board version of the game. For the group from 2021 (Group 2), perfect communication in the team prevails, or it was good or at least improved during the project.

In contrast, the group from 2019 (Group 1) had more or less good communication and only improved over time. Both groups have in common that they have almost zero respondents who would rate the communication as terrible and at the same time did not notice any solution at all. We can take this part of the students as a kind of deviation.

Evaluation of whether the agile game has had an impact on students' understanding of agility is evaluated from two perspectives, from the perspective of the students themselves, based on subjective evaluation and then also objective marks in the exam. According to students, in both cases, the game was very beneficial. As can be seen from Fig. 1, over 80% of students in both cases rated the game as above average to excellent, understanding that they understood at least the basic principles of agile management and Scrum framework.

In 2019, five students were dissatisfied with their role, and in 2021 only three students from an even larger group of students. It is, therefore, possible to say that over the years, the satisfaction and digitization of the game also increase students' satisfaction with the roles they have chosen. It is not so important why the students were satisfied with

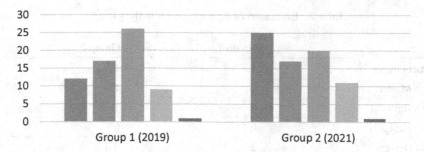

■ Perfect communication between all members during the whole project

■ Very good communication in the beginning, everyone was involved

■ Good communication, rapidly improved during project

■ Bad communication in the beginning, get better during project

■ Terrible communication during whole project

Fig. 1. Communication inside teams

their role, mainly because they chose the role themselves according to their abilities and competencies, which is why it suited them primarily. However, it is more important to analyze why the selected role did not fit the students.

In Table 3, it is possible to see selected roles with which the students were not satisfied in the game for some reason. First, we take a look at Group 1, in this group we had five answers that students were not satisfied with their role. The role that there was no complaint about was Senior Designer. Two students agreed that as Junior Designers they didn't have much work to do and that it was a shame that other roles were more overloaded (for example UX and Senior designer). They didn't have much work, especially at the beginning of the game, but over time this has improved. A UX designer also complained about the role, not because of a lack of work but because of a lack of creativity.

In this case, there was an error in choosing the role. One of the Scrum Masters complained that he also didn't have much work, primarily because the team members didn't take compliance with Scrum seriously.

The last in this group was the Product Owner, who complained that he couldn't lead people, or even in that way. The solution could again be to choose a more appropriate role.

In Group 2, the answers to dissatisfaction with their role were only three students, which is the apparent progress concerning the total number of students in both groups. We had two Junior Designers here who were not satisfied with their role for the same reasons as for Group 1, and that was a lack of work for this role in the game.

The last was UX Designer, who was not satisfied with anything at all and answered the questionnaires unconstructively and almost aggressively critically, so his answers cannot be counted in the research.

Table 3. Evaluation of managing roles in the game.

Role	Group 1	Group 2
Product Owner	1	1
Scrum Master	0	1
UX Designer	0	1
Senior Designer	0	0
Junior Designer	2	2
Number of students	3	5

Table 4. Evaluation of product owners.

Evaluation	PO (2019)	%	PO (2021)	%
1 (the best)	33	52.4	48	64.9
2	20	31.7	18	24.3
3	7	11.1	4	5.4
4	1	1.6	2	2.7
5 (the worst)	2	3.2	2	2.7
Number of students	63	100	74	100

From a communication point of view, the most important roles are the Product Owner (PO) and Scrum Master (SM) roles. As can be seen from the Table 4 and 5, these two positions had a high level of communication.

The vast majority of students evaluated these roles from the point of view of communication very positively to perfectly.

Table 5. Evaluation of scrum masters.

Evaluation	PO (2019)	%	PO (2021)	%
1 (the best)	28	44.4	43	58.1
2	19	30.2	24	32.4
3	9	14.3	6	8.1
4	3	4.8	1	1.4
5 (the worst)	4	6.3	0	0.0
Number of students	63	100	74	100

The group from 2019 rates communication at Scrum Master a little worse than Product Owners by about 4%. In contrast, in the group from 2021, their communication differed really insignificantly to 1%. The difference between Product Owners in both years was almost comparable, it really differed by tenths of a percent, and the same can be said about the comparison of Scrum Masters.

Table 6. Evaluation of senior designers.

Evaluation	SD (2019)	%	SD (2021)	%
1 (the best)	30	47.6	52	70.3
2	26	42.3	19	25.7
3	5	7.8	2	2.7
4	0	0.0	1	1.4
5 (the worst)	2	3.2	0	0.0
Number of students	63	100	74	100

Table 7. Evaluation of UX designers.

Evaluation	UX (2019)	%	UX (2021)	%
1 (the best)	32	50.8	54	73.0
2	23	36.5	16	21.6
3	5	7.9	4	5.4
4	1	1.6	0	0.0
5 (the worst)	2	3.2	0	0.0
Number of students	63	100	74	100

Another evaluated sector was not management positions but positions that perform graphic design, namely Senior Designer (SD) and UX designer (UX) as you can see in Tables 6 and 7. A lack of communication or negative evaluation could be assumed for these roles. However, these roles forced the game to work very closely with the entire team and surprisingly rated this communication as excellent or very good, with some exceptions. Even the mark that means average was scarce here.

Therefore, it can be said that the communication in the team was not affected in any way by the type of game. Paradoxically, communication was generally evaluated better in professional roles, which makes sense in the case of teaching because even to lead and manage people, one must learn. Therefore, it makes sense that communication was paradoxically worse for the leading positions in the game (Fig. 2).

Playing the agile game was also reflected in the overall evaluation of students in the subject of IT Project Management in the field of informatics. This course teaches the basic principles of project management, from product creation, marketing to release to production.

Agile management and various frameworks, including Scrum, which is the most widely used in informatics today, are also taught in this subject. A total of 94 students

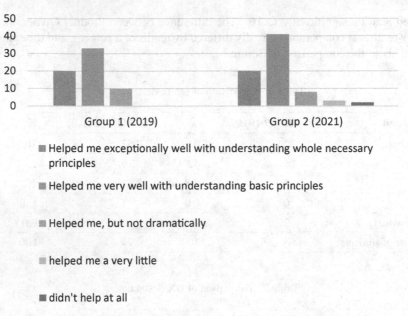

Fig. 2. Evaluation a gain knowledge by students themselves

took part in the exam in 2021. A total of 13 students did not take the exam in due time, only 2 in the first resist and all of them in the following resist.

The overall statistics can be seen in the table in the "Group 2021" column. Only one student did not pass the exam, and the vast majority of students were graded 1 or 2, which is a very positive result (Table 8).

Table 8. Evaluation based on exam

Evaluation	Group 1	%	Group 2	%
1 – excellent	29	46.0	33	34.4
2 – very good	29	46.0	45	46.9
3 – good	5	7.9	15	15.8
4 – insufficiently	0	0.0	3	3.1
Number of students	63	100	96	100

On the other hand, students from group 2019 had a more positive evaluation, but the vast majority of students did so from both groups. In the case of the group from 2019, only one student did not pass the exam in due time. An essential part of the overall evaluation was the oral exam. It is possible to say unequivocally that the students who did not take the exam did not do it mainly due to questions outside the field of agility and Scrum.

In contrast to the group from 2018, which did not play agile in any form, many students here had a worsened evaluation mainly because of issues in the field of agile management and agile frameworks, including the just mentioned Scrum (Fig. 3).

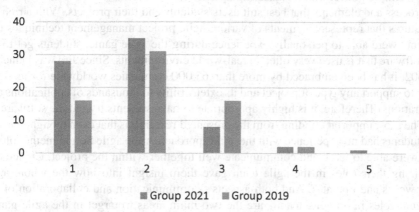

Fig. 3. Evaluating the agile game by students

Lastly, it is necessary to evaluate the students themselves, how satisfied they were with the agile game in the classroom. As can be seen from the chart above, the vast majority of students liked the game very much and overall found it very beneficial and fun. According to students, the most significant disadvantages of the agile game include roles and authorities, their description, sometimes overlapping competencies, etc.

According to the students, the second disadvantage was the lack of time to complete all tasks, but some students rated this as an advantage because the point of the game was also for students to try working under time pressure, as is the practice case. The last thing that should definitely not be overlooked was the reminder from the students that it would be good to do a sample demo of the game, including one sprint played. The students really liked that they could try agile project management and projects in the IT sector in general on a practical example, including practical tools used in practice, such as JIRA. They also saw learning to work in a team and working under time pressure as an advantage. Overall, the students rated the game very positively.

4   Discussion

The simple agile game, which is based on the authors' previous research Havazík and Pavlíčková [4, 5], was first designed and played as a desk game in 2019. Based on this experience, authors continued their research and in the context of the Covid 19 pandemic and the impossibility of playing the game in the classroom, an online version was designed in software tools JIRA and JunoOne [5, 6]. Based on this research using the Jira software tool, the game was played in the autumn of 2021 with students of the Master's degree in Computer Science in the IT Project Management course at the Faculty of Economics and Management of the Czech University of Live Sciences Prague.

Based on the results mentioned above, students liked the combination of the Scrum framework and Jira software because Jira software brings them closer to the real environment of agile projects. Jira software embraces a truly agile approach by providing users a simple platform that is also highly customizable. Jira software can implement the process and elements that best suit users/students and their projects. With a rich set of features that represent elements of various agile project management techniques that students were able to personally experience during the agile game, students got to try out software that is used very often in real-world environments. Since Jira was launched in 2002, it has been embraced by more than 65,000 companies worldwide for its flexibility to support any type of project and its extensibility to thousands of applications and integrations. Therefore, it is highly appropriate to have students try out the software.

The most important finding from the presented research is that even though many of the students had no experience with the agile approach or the agile Scrum methodology, they were able to work and communicate well together within the project. Choice and practicing their roles in the agile team gave them insight into how the whole agile team works and operates. And both aspects - communication and collaboration of the different roles in an agile team - are the two main areas to target in the agile games (games designed for teaching agile approach) for the future because they incorporate the elements of reality into the study of project management.

It is significantly more effective to include real elements into the learning of agile methodology. Therefore, it seems to be very appropriate to include elements of risk - drawing lots of unpredictable situations that students had to react to during the game and that could be treated in the risk analysis - also, in this way, students practiced real situations and gained preparation for future deployment in the real practice of IT project management. Similar results - preparation for future deployment in the real practice and effect on job performance - demonstrate Yilmaz and O'Connor [16] in their gamification of the Scrum methodology in real software development.

Teaching agile methodology using Jira is highly beneficial. Jira is widely used mainly by IT developers (that's why students played the agile game of developing a comprehensive IT project - web design, mobile application, etc.), and other teams of agile projects. Jira helps them to have a clear idea of the workflow regardless of the different methodologies used; in our case, Scrum was used. Jira, because it supports both web and mobile apps, makes it easy for team leaders to know the status and act on different levels of complexity. This maintains a balance in the agile framework. Since Jira includes many task-related flows, the manager can easily implement any other team dependency with the ongoing project.

Using Jira, students could also try out deadline tracking. Each team member had an overview of deadlines and task priorities. This kept the whole team informed and allowed them to complete tasks on time. Jira works with various APIs to help customers collaborate with the issue tracking system. Thus, the students were able to enjoy the Jira interface both on PC and as a mobile application. This allowed students to become more familiar with Agile and the Jira software. Students are then better prepared for future practice in IT project management.

However, this approach assumes at least a minimal knowledge of Jira software. Alternatively, agile game participants need to be trained in this software. A weakness of the authors' presented game is its required preparation and familiarization with the scope of the IT project they are developing in the game.

Nevertheless, the game presented can be considered beneficial for learning the basic principles of agile project management.

5 Conclusion

This paper shows that teaching agile methodology through games is very beneficial and positively evaluated among students (participants in games). They particularly liked the use of Jira software, which is now widely used for project management in IT sector in real practice. Thus, both games train students in the basic understanding of agile methodology and the second game using Jira also teaches them the basic use of this software.

Both introduced games increase students' ability to collaborate and communicate in a team, which are the main principles not only of agile methodologies but also of the whole project management.

Although the results of the two types of games played have been evaluated very positively, both by students and teachers, the authors recommend the second type of game, with Jira software. This second game reflects more the real project management environment.

It is also evident that students who played the agile game (of any type) were better at answering questions related to agility and the Scrum framework and were more successful in the final oral exam of the subject IT project management.

The presented method of teaching in the form of a game can be considered useful for teaching the basic principles of agile approach.

Acknowledgement. The results and knowledge included herein have been obtained owing to support from the following institutional grants. Internal grant agency of the Faculty of Economics and Management, Czech University of Life Sciences in Prague, grant no. 2019A0008, "Analýza týmových rolí v IT projektech pomocí speciální hry AGILNĚ".

References

1. Anslow, C., Maurer, F.: An experience report at teaching a group based agile software development project course. In: SIGCSE 2015 - Proceedings of the 46th ACM Technical Symposium on Computer Science Education, (Cmmi), pp. 500–505 (2015). https://doi.org/10.1145/2676723.2677284
2. Boehm, B., Grunbacher, P., Briggs, R.O.: Developing groupware for requirements negotiation: lessons learned. IEEE Softw. **18**(3), 46–55 (2001)
3. Campbell, J., Kurkovsky, S., Liew, Ch.W., Tafliovich, A.: Scrum and agile methods in software engineering courses. In: 47th ACM Technical Symposium on Computing Science Education, Memphis, TN, USA (2016)
4. Havazik, O., Pavlíčková, P.: Using a simulation game in the education. In: Proceedings of the 17th International Conference Efficiency and Responsibility in Education 2020 (ERIE 2020), pp. 76–82 (2020)

5. Havazik, O., Pavlickova, P.: How to design Agile game for education purposes in JIRA, pp. 331–334 (2020). https://doi.org/10.1109/codit49905.2020.9263937
6. Havazík, O., Pavlíčková, P., Pavlíček, J.: Agile Game in Online Environment. In: Polyvyanyy, A., Rinderle-Ma, S. (eds.) CAiSE 2021. LNBIP, vol. 423, pp. 17–25. Springer, Cham (2021). https://doi.org/10.1007/978-3-030-79022-6_2
7. Kropp, M., Meier, A.: Teaching agile software development at university level: values, management, and craftsmanship. In: Software Engineering Education Conference, Proceedings, (May), pp. 179–188 (2013). https://doi.org/10.1109/CSEET.2013.6595249
8. Kurkovsky, S.: A simple game to introduce scrum concepts. In: 51st ACM Technical Symposium on Computer Science Education (SIGCSE 2020), 11–14 March 2020, Portland, OR, USA. ACM, New York (2020). https://doi.org/10.1145/3328778.3372593
9. López-Martínez, J., Juárez-Ramírez, R., Huertas, C., Jiménez, S., Guerra-García, C.: Problems in the adoption of agile-scrum methodologies: a systematic literature review. In: 4th International Conference in Software Engineering Research and Innovation, Puebla, México (2016). https://doi-org.infozdroje.czu.cz/10.1109/conisoft.2016.30
10. Mayor, J., López-Fernández, D.: Scrum VR: virtual reality serious video game to learn scrum. Appl. Sci. **11**, 9015 (2021). https://doi.org/10.3390/app11199015
11. Pinto, L., et al.: On the use of scrum for the management of practcal projects in graduate courses. In: Proceedings - Frontiers in Education Conference, FIE (2009). https://doi.org/10.1109/FIE.2009.5350404
12. Przybyłek, A., Albecka, M., Springer, O., et al.: Game-based Sprint retrospectives: multiple action research. Empir. Software Eng. **27**(1), 1–56 (2022). https://doi.org/10.1007/s10664-021-10043-z
13. Schwaber, K.: Agile Project Management with scrum. Microsoft Press, Redmond (2004)
14. Schwaber, K., Sutherland, J.: The Scrum GuideTM The Definitive Guide to Scrum: The Rules of the Game (2017)
15. Sutherland, J.: The Scrum papers (2022). http://jeffsutherland.com/scrumpapers.pdf
16. Yilmaz, M., O'Connor, R.V.: A scrumban integrated gamification approach to guide software process improvement: a Turkish case study. Tehnicki Vjesnik **23**(1), 237–245 (2016). https://doi.org/10.17559/TV-20140922220409

Formulation of Agile Business Rules for Purchasing Control System Components Process Improvement

A. Maron(iD) and M. Maron(✉)(iD)

National Research University Higher School of Economics, Moscow, Russia
{amaron,mmaron}@hse.ru

Abstract. Purpose: The relevance of the study is due to the fact that when purchasing on the international market it is extremely important to choose a supplier, when working with which the risks associated with the volatility of exchange rates will be minimized. The situation is now changing rapidly. In connection with these companies need reasonable flexible business rules for solving this problem.

Design/Methodology/Approach: Methods of decision theory under uncertainty were applied to solve the problem. Moreover, for uncertainty, which cannot be estimated using the methods of probability theory. The decision is based on Savage 's Criteria - Criteria of Minimum Maximum Risk.

Findings: Formulas for calculating the minimum maximum risk when working with suppliers and the amount and the rule for the rational choice of both the supplier and the moment of purchase have been obtained.

Practical Implication: Based on the obtained formulas, flexible business rules for choosing a supplier and purchasing moments have been created.

Value: The result is of particular interest to managers responsible for the procurement of components in the international market.

Keywords: Agile business rules · Risk minimization · Control system

1 Substantial Statement of the Problem

An agile approach of project management was a natural response to the limitations build in the classical mathematical model of project management. This model, and the associated critical path method, does not assume existence of scenarios. At the same time, the project, by definition, is a unique entity. There is an obvious contradiction. The manager is asked to create an accurate work plan in the context of complete or partial lack of experience in achieving the set result. Note that the GERT method was the first answer to this contradiction. It can be considered the forerunner of the agile approach to project management. An agile approach is necessary not only for project management, but also for the successful management of business processes in an unstable environment. Business processes are often contrasted with projects because the project is unique, and the business process is repeatable. At the same time, both are a sequence of works carried out according to a certain plan. Also, both are special cases of an operation - a set of

© The Author(s), under exclusive license to Springer Nature Switzerland AG 2022
E. Babkin et al. (Eds.): MOBA 2022, LNBIP 457, pp. 41–49, 2022.
https://doi.org/10.1007/978-3-031-17728-6_4

measures aimed at achieving goals. Moreover, they have similar mathematical models. The analogy between the net-work model of the project and the business process models in IDEF3 and eEPC notations is especially obvious. However, notations for developing business process models have elements of the "OR" type to indicate a possible change in a business process, considering certain circumstances. Business process models were created several decades later than the classic project model. The problems arising from the lack of flexibility in them were taken into account.

Manufacturing companies operate in an environment of supply and demand uncertainty, leading to price volatility. For them, flexibility in managing business processes is not only and not so much a change in the sequence of work in business processes, but the presence of decisive rules that allow rational decisions to be made. It is highly desirable that these rules be based on a strict, yet practicable, mathematical approach. In this paper, this approach is proposed for the first time for solving the following problem.

Consider a company that manufactures blocks for a train control system. Blocks are produced in large quantities. They are installed on locomotives. Microcontrollers are needed to produce blocks. The base price for the microcontroller is set in one of the reserve currencies. Possible suppliers are available. They are in different countries. The buyer should take into account that the conversion of the currency of his country into the final currency of the purchase will take place in two stages. First, convert to the currency of the supplier's country. Then, converting the supplier's currency into the purchase currency. In addition, the price of the microcontroller for each supplier may differ from the base one. The company knows how many microcontrollers it must purchase per month to meet the production plan. Purchase for a month can be carried out in two stages: at the beginning of the month and in the middle. At the beginning of the month, the conversion rates are known. The rates that will be in the middle of the month are not exactly known. However, it is possible to predict the ranges of their change. The company wants to spend as little of its country's currency on the purchase as possible. To do this, it is necessary to choose the right moments of purchase and supplier in the world market. An urgent task is to create flexible rules for making such a choice. This problem is solved in this work on the basis of Savage 's criterion - the criterion of minimum maximum risk. Work (Maron and Maron 2019) is the main work on the basis of which the solution was obtained.

2 Mathematical Problem Definition

The company must purchase a certain number of microcontrollers. There are n possible suppliers on the international market. The sum S_i is known in the purchase currency that will be required to purchase the entire batch of controllers from supplier i (i = 1, 2, ..., n). The purchase can be carried out in two stages: at the beginning of the month (the instant t_0) and in the middle of the month (the instant t_1). The company pays in the currency of its country. The conversion takes place in two stages. First, convert to the currency of the supplier's country. Then, converting the supplier's currency into the purchase currency. At the instant t_0 for the unit of buyer's currency he can receive a_{0i} units of the i supplier's currency. At the instant t_0 supplier i can receive b_{0i} units of the purchase currency. Both conversion rates at instant t_1 are unknown. However, it can be assumed that they are within $[a_i; A_i]$ and $[b_i; B_i]$, respectively.

It is required to build flexible business rules for the rational determination of the supplier and the moments of purchase from him.

3 Results

To solve the problem, it is necessary to determine the optimality criterion.

In this case it is expedient to apply game theory methods, namely decision-making methods in the conditions of indeterminacy which cannot be estimated by means of probability theory methods to the solution of a task (Dominiak 2006; Dominiak 2009]. There are two main criteria of a decision making in such situations: the criterion of the Wald (Wenzel 2018) and the criterion of Savage (Somasundaram and Diecidue 2018; Cohen et al. 2009) although other criteria are sometimes used (Achelis 2000) as for example, the criterion of Hurwitz. According to criterion of the Wald strategy at which the minimum prize is maximum is optimum. It is a criterion of "the poor pessimist" who considers that conditions of carrying out operation will be the inferior for it, and at the same time it is necessary to receive the small, but the guaranteed prize (Anderson and Gerbing 1988; Anderson and Faff 2008].

The criterion of Savage is based on a concept of risk. The risk, by the definition of Savage, is the difference between that prize which we could receive if we foreknew with what there will be conditions of carrying out operation, and the prize which will be received from the application of the chosen strategy. According to the criterion of Savage, the optimum strategy at which the maximum risk is minimum. It is a criterion of the pessimist, but the pessimist is too rich considering that the most terrible outcome is to miss a prize. In our case the decision based on the Savage criterion, will not allow the considerable deviations from the minimum possible sum necessary for the purchase (Bettman et al. 2009; Bettman et al. 2006). We accept the Savage criterion as an optimality criterion for solving the problem.

In the work of (Maron and Maron 2019) solved the following problem. Today (in t_0 instant) the company has money in euro. Today's selling rate of euro for rubles is equal to E_0 [RUB/EUR]. Tomorrow (in t_1 instant) the company needs to pay S sum in rubles. Tomorrow's course is unknown. However, there are bases to assume that it will change ranging from E_{min} to E_{max} and

$$E_0 \epsilon [E_{min}; E_{max}] \tag{1}$$

It is required to define what part of tools in euro to sell today, and what tomorrow for obtaining the required sum of money in rubles.

Let's x quantity of euro sold today at course E_0. Proven that the minimum of the maximum risk is reached in a point x, where

$$x\left(1 - \frac{E_0}{E_{min}}\right) + S\left(\frac{1}{E_{min}} - \frac{1}{E_0}\right) = x\left(1 - \frac{E_0}{E_{max}}\right) \tag{2}$$

This optimal point is

$$x^* = \frac{E_{max}(E_0 - E_{min})}{E_0^2(E_{max} - E_{min})} S \tag{3}$$

In relation to our case when buying through a supplier i.

$$E_0 = a_{0i}b_{0i}; \; E_{min} = a_ib_i; \; E_{max} = A_iB_i; \; S = S_i. \tag{4}$$

Let us substitute (3) into (2). Consider (4) we obtain the following expression for the minimum of the maximum risk of purchasing microcontrollers through supplier i

$$R_i = \frac{(a_{0i}b_{0i} - a_ib_i)(A_iB_i - a_{0i}b_{0i})}{a_{0i}^2 b_{0i}^2 (A_iB_i - a_ib_i)} S_i \tag{5}$$

The most difficult to choose is the case when for all i the condition like condition (1) is satisfied

$$a_{0i}b_{0i} \in [a_ib_i; \; A_iB_i] \tag{6}$$

The results obtained allow us to formulate flexible business rules for choosing a supplier and purchasing moments for this most important case. These are the rules.

1. Determine the supplier for which the value of R_i is minimal.
2. Let's say this is a supplier with number k. At the beginning of the month, spend the amount on the purchase of microcontrollers

$$x_k^* = \frac{A_kB_k(a_{0k}b_{0k} - a_kb_k)}{a_{0k}^2 b_{0k}^2 (A_kB_k - a_kb_k)} S_k \tag{7}$$

In the middle of the month, buy in addition for the remaining required amount at the actual rates on the date of purchase.

4   Example

There are two possible suppliers. One in China. One in India. Final price in US dollars (USD) offered by them: 1 200 000 USD and 1 050 000 USD, respectively. Purchase through the first supplier (i = 1) requires preliminary conversion of Russian rubles (RUR) into yuan (CNY). A purchase through a second supplier (i = 2) involves the preliminary conversion of Russian rubles into Indian rupees (INR).

Rates at the beginning of the month: $a_{01} = 0.0611$ [CNY/RUR],
$a_{02} = 0.7353$ [INR/RUR], $b_{01} = 0.1575$ [USD/CNY],
$b_{02} = 0.0131$ [USD/INR].

Expected ranges of change by the middle of the month: CNY/RUR - [0.0525; 0.0688], CNY/USD - [0.1567; 0.1575],

INR/RUR - [0.5495; 0.9009], INR/USD - [0.0131; 0.0132].

It is required to determine the best supplier and the amount in rubles that should be spent on the purchase at the beginning of the month.

First, we make sure that condition (6) is satisfied for both suppliers.

Let's use the proposed flexible business rule.

1. Using the formula (5), we determine the minimax risks of buying from the first and second suppliers. We have $R_1 = 8\ 397\ 017$ RUR; $R_2 = 13\ 264\ 368$ RUR.
2. We decide to purchase microcontrollers through a supplier from China.
3. According to formula (7), we determine the amount that should be spent on the purchase at the beginning of the month. It will make $x_1^* = 75\ 068\ 418$ RUR.

This is one of the examples of practical calculations that are made by the proposed method. The effectiveness of the proposed method was evaluated. The verification procedure is as follows. The minimum amount of money for which it would be possible to buy the required number of microcontrollers is determined knowing exchange rate by the middle of the month. This value is compared with the actual amount spent in organizing the purchase in accordance with the specified method. For thirty purchases, the average value of the difference was no more than 10%. A theoretical comparison was also made with the following approaches.

1. Always buy at the beginning of the month from the supplier offering the lowest price in the final currency.
2. Always buy from the supplier that offers the lowest price in the final currency and determine the moment of purchase of the all amount of supplies by "coin toss" method.

In both cases, the average deviation from the minimum flow rate was more than 25%. Therefore, it can be argued that the proposed method is effective.

5 Discussion

For any manufacturing company, the fight against price volatility is one of the key tasks. If the risk management system is not working effectively, then the company will face a lot of difficulties from customer dissatisfaction and pricing problems to blunders in budget planning and reduced profitability of the production process. Before building and analyzing mathematical models to determine the optimal procurement plan, it is necessary to accurately classify the risk associated with price volatility, as well as identify common strategies for minimizing it. From an economic and financial perspective, this risk can be considered as a financial one, since it has a significant impact on the economic performance of the company, as well as on the cash flow of the organization (Allen 2012). To minimize this risk, there are three main strategies (Gaudenzi et al. 2018): search strategies, contracting strategies, and financial strategies. When applying the first strategy, the company can influence the timing, quantity and type of raw materials to minimize the impact of price volatility. The second approach involves the development of a priori contracts with suppliers in the event of a sharp change in prices. Funding strategies use commodity exchanges with third-party financial instruments such as futures and options. One of the most common is the "term of purchase" method (Johnson et al. 2021). The content of this approach is that if a price increase is expected, then the manager makes purchases at a given time. If there is a tendency to reduce prices in the future, then the purchase of raw materials can be waited, provided that the necessary reserves are available. To solve the problem of purchasing raw materials and optimizing the level of stocks in the search for the optimal terms of purchases, two main approaches can be used - probabilistic and statistical decision methods. Further, the main mathematical models proposed in the framework of these two approaches, as well as their possible disadvantages and advantages, are considered.

The development of the probabilistic approach began with the consideration of basic models of procurement and inventory management with a fixed demand and a known purchase price. Further, the main focus of the study turned to the optimization of stocks with an unknown demand for the final product. The literature on this topic is quite extensive. Let's look at a few examples. Weinott and Wagner (1965) in their work considered a dynamic stocks model, in which the demand for a product is described by a discrete random variable. The main goal of this work was to create an efficient procedure for calculating the optimal (s, S) policy. With this strategy, an order for suppliers is placed when the stocks have reached the level s. The order volume is determined by the deviation of the current level from the level S. Zheng Yu-Sheng (Zheng 1991) in his paper presented a simple proof of this policy (s, S) in an infinite horizon stocks system. Also, developments on this topic, including optimization of the calculation of the upper and lower bounds and the definition of the cost function, are presented in the works of Fabian (Fabian et al. 1959), Zheng and Federgrun (1991), Archibald and Silver (1978], Bell (1970], Eaglehart (1961), Sahin (1982) and Stidham (1977).

In comparison, the literature on the topic of this work (the purchase price of reserves is not known) is relatively less (Kim et al. 2015]. Morris (1959) took one of the first steps towards solving this problem in 1959. He considered two possible probabilistic approaches to solve it: making one purchase before a certain deadline and a general purchasing strategy in which the volume is presented as a function of the price and the number of days until the end of the current period of purchases. Another approach was proposed by Herbert Scarfe [21] in 1960, applying the (s, S) model to the purchasing problem under price volatility. Kalimon in 1971 extended this work by proving the optimality of this policy and defining s and S as functions of the purchase price and the number of remaining periods. In his work, he considered the following two cases: the case of a finite period of purchases and the case of an infinite period of purchases. Vangelis F. Magirow went further and considered a purchasing model with storage restrictions and found the optimal policy under conditions of constant demand. A feature of this model is that the price of raw materials is described by a random process. Another feature is storage volume accounting, which can be useful for estimating the optimal storage capacity. All of these methods consider the procurement plan taking into account a large number of constraints, which makes them more realistic and applicable for drawing up a procurement plan. At the same time, they have one big drawback: to build models based on a probabilistic approach, a fairly accurate estimate of the probabilistic distribution of prices for future periods is required. Predicting a continuous probability distribution with the accuracy needed to model a procurement plan is a time-consuming and labor-consuming task for an organization. For this reason, Morris [20] proposed a "dollar averaging" strategy that frees the buyer from predicting future price fluctuations. This strategy assumes that the same amount is spent on each purchase. There are other approaches that go away from predicting the possible spectrum of price fluctuations and focus on minimizing risk.

A huge number of works in the field of investment is devoted to pass from one tool into another (Lewellen 2004; Lo et al. 2000). In most of them need of a transition based on prediction of change of cost of tools is required (Dichev and Tang 2009; Weller et al. 2007]. Others refer to financial crises and how the market reacts (Thalassinos and Thalassinos 2018; Polyakova et al. 2019). Usually we apply the technical analysis, the fundamental analysis or their combination to prediction (Fabozzi and Peterson 2003; Groenewald and Pretorius 2011). The technical analysis is an attempt to predict the future on the basis of the past taking into account the mass behavior of players in the market (Marshall et al. 2007; Gaspars-Wieloch 2012).

The apparatus of the technical analysis is very diverse. In it both a simple visual method, and the most difficult numerical method of successive approximations used is neural networks (Swanson et al. 2003; Haykin 2008). First of all the technical analysis is applied at a game of share and the foreign exchange markets where there are larger arrays of historical data. There are a lot of researchers skeptically fall into technical analysis (Fama and French 2006; Basili et al. 2008). They call into question a possibility of prediction of the future from the past without an explanation of the structure of this phenomenon (Chronopoulos et al. 2011). The fundamental analysis is based on the economic theory and explains the reasons of changes of cost of tools, but the accuracy of these predictions is not always sufficient for the adoption of the justified decisions (Beneish et al. 2001; Aaker 1991). Game theory methods are also applied first of all in the theory of formation of an optimal portfolio of investments. The classical approach here is Markovits's theory.

The difference of the considered task from the tasks solved earlier consists that currency exchange on the given short price is obligatory. Respectively it is necessary to execute it in the best way.

6 Conclusion

The most valuable result is the following. It is proposed to make a decision based on the prediction of ranges of exchange rates. This is practically feasible, in contrast to the forecast of exchange rates. Moreover, the result is stable. Small changes in the boundaries of the predicted ranges do not dramatically affect the result!

7 Recommendation

The result is of particular interest to managers responsible for the procurement of components in the international market.

References

Aaker, D.A.: Managing Brand Equity. The Free Press, New York (1991)
Achelis, S.: Technical Analysis from A to Z, 2nd edn., p. 400. McGraw-Hill, New York (2000)

Anderson, J.C., Gerbing, D.W.: Structural equation modeling in practice: a review and recommended two-step approach. Psychol. Bull. **103**(3), 411 (1988)

Allen, S.L.: Financial Risk Management: A Practitioner's Guide to Managing Market and Credit Risk. John Wiley & Sons, New York. T. 721 (2012)

Anderson, J., Faff, R.: Point and figure charting: a computational methodology and trading rule performance in the S&P 500 futures market. Int. Rev. Financ. Anal. **17**(1), 198–217 (2008)

Archibald, B.C., Silver, E.A.: (s, S) policies under continuous review and discrete compound Poisson demand. Manage. Sci. **24**(9), 899–909 (1978)

Basili, M., Chateauneuf, A., Fontini, F.: Precautionary principle as a rule of choice with optimism on windfall gains and pessimism on catastrophic losses. Ecol. Econ. **67**, 485–491 (2008)

Bell, C.E.: Improved algorithms for inventory and replacement-stocking problems. SIAM J. Appl. Math. **18**(3), 558–566 (1970)

Beneish, M., Lee, C.M., Tarpley, R.L.: Contextual fundamental analysis through the prediction of extreme returns. Rev. Acc. Stud. **6**, 165–189 (2001)

Bettman, J., Sault, S., Welch, E.: Fundamental and technical analysis: substitutes or compliments? SSRN Electron. J. 28 (2006)

Bettman, J., Salut, S., Schultz, E.: Fundamental and technical analysis, substitutes of compliments. Acc. Financ. **49**, 21–36 (2009)

Chronopoulos, M., De Reyck, B., Siddiqui, A.: Optimal investment under operational flexibility, risk aversion, and uncertainty. Eur. J. Oper. Res. **213**, 221–237 (2011)

Cohen, R., Polk, C., Vuolteenaho, T.: The price is (almost) right. J. Financ. **64**(6), 2739–2782 (2009)

Dichev, I.L., Tang, V.W.: Earnings volatility and earnings predictability. J. Account. Econ. **47**, 160–181 (2009)

Dominiak, C.: Multicriteria decision aid under uncertainty. In: Trzaskalik, T. (ed.) Multiple Criteria Decision Making 2005, pp. 63–82. Publisher of the Karol Adamiecki University of Economics in Katowice (2006)

Dominiak, C.: Multicriteria decision aiding procedure under risk and uncertainty. In: Trzaskalik, T. (ed.) Multiple Criteria Decision Making 2008, pp. 61–88. Publisher of the Karol Adamiecki University of Economics in Katowice (2009)

Fabian, T., et al.: Purchasing raw material on a fluctuating market. Oper. Res. **7**(1), 107–122 (1959)

Fabozzi, F., Peterson, F.: Financial Management and Analysis, p. 1007. Wiley & Sons, NY (2003)

Fama, E.F., French, K.R.: Profitability, investment, and average returns. J. Financ. Econ. **82**, 491–518 (2006)

Gaspars-Wieloch, H.: Limited efficiency of optimization methods in solving economic decision problems. Ekonomista **3**, 303–324 (2012)

Gaudenzi, B., et al.: An exploration of factors influencing the choice of commodity price risk mitigation strategies. J. Purchas. Suppl. Manag. **24**(3), 218–237 (2018)

Groenewald, M.E., Pretorius, P.D.: Comparison of decision making under uncertainty investment strategies with the money market. J. Financ. Stud. Res. **2011**(2011), 16 (2011)

Haykin, S.: Neural Networks and Learning Machines. 3rd Edn. Pearson, London, 936 (2008)

Iglehart, D.L.: Dynamic programming and stationary analyses of inventory problems. Stanford Univ Calif Applied Mathematics and Statistics Labs (1961)

Johnson, F., et al.: Purchasing and supply management. McGraw-Hill Companies, Inc., New York (2021)

Kim, K.K., Liu, J., Lee, C.G.: A stochastic inventory model with price quotation. IIE Trans. **47**(8), 851–864 (2015)

Lewellen, J.: Predicting returns with financial ratios. J. Financ. Econ. **74**, 209–235 (2004)

Lo, A.W., Mamaysky, H., Wang, J.: Foundations of technical analysis: computational algorithms, statistical inference, and empirical implementation. J. Financ. **55**(4), 1705–1765 (2000)

Maron, A., Maron, M.: Minimizing the maximum risk of currency conversion for a company buying abroad. Eur. Res. Stud. J. **22**(3), 59–67 (2019)

Marshall, B.R., Young, M., Rose, L.C.: Market timing with candlestick technical analysis. J. Financ. Transf. Capco Inst. **20**, 18–25 (2007)

Morris, W.T.: Some analysis of purchasing policy. Manag. Sci. **5**(4), 443–452 (1959)

Polyakova, A.G., Loginov, M.P., Serebrennikova, A.I., Thalassinos, E.I.: Design of a socio-economic processes monitoring system based on network analysis and big data. Int. J. Econ. Bus. Adm. **7**(1), 130–139 (2019)

Sahin, I.: On the objective function behavior in (s, S) inventory models. Oper. Res. **30**(4), 709–724 (1982)

Sniedovich, M.: Wald's maximin model: a treasure in disguise. J. Risk Financ. **9**, 287–291 (2008)

Stidham, S., Jr.: Cost models for stochastic clearing systems. Oper. Res. **25**(1), 100–127 (1977)

Somasundaram, J., Diecidue, E.: Regret theory and risk attitudes. J. Risk Uncertain. **55**(2–3), 147–175 (2018). https://doi.org/10.1007/s11166-017-9268-9

Swanson, E.P., Rees, L., Juarez-Valdes, L.F.: The contribution of fundamental analysis after a currency devaluation. Account. Rev. **78**(3), 875–902 (2003)

Thalassinos, I.E., Thalassinos, E.Y.: Financial Crises and e-Commerce: How Are they related? SSRN (2018). https://ssrn.com/abstract=3330169

Veinott, A.F., Jr., Wagner, H.M.: Computing optimal (s, S) inventory policies. Manag. Sci. **11**(5), 525–552 (1965)

Weller, P., Friesen, G., Dunham, L.: Price trends and patterns in technical analysis: a theoretical and empirical examination. J. Bank. Financ. **33**(6), 1089–1100 (2007)

Wenzel, E.: Research operatsiy : zadachi , printsipy , metodologiya (in Russian). KnoRus, 192 p. (2018)

Zheng, Y.S.: A simple proof for optimality of (s, S) policies in infinite-horizon inventory systems. J. Appl. Probabi. 28, 802–810 (1991)

Zheng, Y.S., Federgruen, A.: Finding optimal (s, S) policies is about as simple as evaluating a single policy. Oper. Res. **39**(4), 654–665 (1991)

A Business Intelligence Tool
for Explaining Similarity

Simona Colucci[1]([✉]), Francesco M. Donini[2], Nicola Iurilli[1],
and Eugenio Di Sciascio[1]

[1] Politecnico di Bari, Bari, Italy
{simona.colucci,eugenio.disciascio}@poliba.it,
n.iurilli@studenti.poliba.it
[2] Universitá degli Studi della Tuscia, Viterbo, Italy
donini@unitus.it

Abstract. Agile Business often requires to identify similar objects
(firms, providers, end users, products) between an older business domain
and a newer one. Data-driven tools for aggregating similar resources are
nowadays often used in Business Intelligence applications, and a large
majority of them involve Machine Learning techniques based on similarity metrics. However effective, the mathematics such tools are based
on does not lend itself to human-readable explanations of their results,
leaving a manager using them in a "take it as is"-or-not dilemma. To
increase trust in such tools, we propose and implement a general method
to explain the similarity of a given group of RDF resources. Our tool
is based on the theory of Least Common Subsumers (LCS), and can be
applied to every domain requiring the comparison of RDF resources,
including business organizations. Given a set of RDF resources found
to be similar by Data-driven tools, we first compute the LCS of the
resources, which is a generic RDF resource describing the features shared
by the group recursively—*i.e.,* at any depth in feature paths. Subsequently, we translate the LCS in English common language. Being agnostic to the aggregation criteria, our implementation can be pipelined with
every other aggregation tool. To prove this, we cascade an implementation of our method to *(i)* the comparison of contracting processes in
Public Procurement (using TheyBuyForYou), and *(ii)* the comparison
and clustering of drugs (using k-Means) in Drugbank. For both applications, we present a fairly readable description of the commonalities of
the cluster given as input.

Keywords: Explainable Artificial Intelligence (XAI) · Resource
Description Framework (RDF) · Least Common Subsumer (LCS)

1 Introduction

The ability of a business organization to rapidly adapt to changing conditions—
referred to as Agility—often requires, among other needs, a rapid identification

E. Babkin et al. (Eds.): MOBA 2022, LNBIP 457, pp. 50–64, 2022.
https://doi.org/10.1007/978-3-031-17728-6_5

of pairs—or clusters—of similar objects, being they partners, products, requirements, etc. This problem has been widely investigated in the literature and
applied to heterogeneous application domains, ranging from business strategy
[20], to manufacturing [10] to drug analysis [9], among others.

Aggregating similar entities in a large dataset may reveal patterns, point out
special groups, and in general it helps in understanding data. Data-driven tools
for aggregating resources by some similarity measure are nowadays available by
the dozens [7,14], and a large majority of them involve Machine Learning techniques based on similarity metrics. However, the mathematics such tools are
based on is rather complex, therefore approaches that make the tool transparent in order to explain a user how the cluster was constructed do not lead to
human-readable explanations. This problem leaves to the manager using the tool
the burden to make explicit which characteristics are similar in the aggregated
resources—a task which is not always self-evident.

We provide a method for describing the commonalities among a given set of
RDF resources, that can be pipelined to any tool for clusterization whose output
is one or more cluster of RDF resources judged similar by the tool. Since our
method is logic-based, it can abstract with blank nodes features that, although
different, lead to a common value through a recursive chain (see Sect. 3 for more
details).

As a byproduct, our method can be used also in a fine-tuning phase of a
clusterizing tool, since it allows one to immediately identify which clusters are
significant—among the ones obtained—for a human reader and possibly which
features in the data lead to significant clusterization.

The rest of this paper is organized as follows: in the next section, we report
related work on Natural Language Generation for RDF. Section 3 recalls main
notions about the definition of LCS in RDF. In Sect. 4, we show our logic-based
method for the explanation of the similarity of RDF resources. We demonstrate
the feasibility of our approach by showing its results in two different contexts in
Sect. 5. Conclusions close the paper.

2   Related Work

The need for making explicit the interpretation of clustering results emerged
a long time ago. In 1980, in fact, conceptual clustering [12] was introduced as
the problem of returning clusters of resources, together with a concept explaining the proposed aggregation. In the meanwhile, several conceptual clustering
approaches and algorithms have been proposed, the most influential of which
have been reviewed in a recent work by Pérez-Suárez et al. [13]. None of the
approaches summarized by Pérez-Suárez et al. deals with RDF resources. An
approach to conceptual clustering of RDF resources based on LCS was proposed
by Colucci et al. [6].

Our proposal stems from a similar need, but, differently from works in the
field of conceptual clustering, we do not build clusters of RDF resources; we focus
only on their explanation. To this aim, we propose a logic-based methodology:

the natural language text explaining the cluster is generated from the set of RDF triples computed as the LCS of all cluster items, which abstracts the commonalities of all resources.

The problem of generating Natural Language text from Semantic Web (SW) data has been widely addressed in the literature and continues to represent a relevant research topic. A systematic review of main approaches up to 2014 was conducted by Bouayad-Agha *et al.* [1] who classify at least 11 Natural Language Generation (NLG) approaches working on RDF graphs, w.r.t. to several features, including the verbalization request (part of the input graph to verbalize) and the communicative goal (information to return). Possible communicative goals are: returning all facts in the verbalization request, returning a user-selected set of facts, returning the most typical facts, returning the most relevant facts. Apparently, no research work is able to generate text from derived triples not explicitly stated in RDF and to manage anonymous resources. Bouayad-Agha *et al.* [1] also point out the need for summarizing information among challenging communicative goals.

The current research trend, to the best of our knowledge, is mostly focused on improving the readability of textual descriptions generated from RDF, w.r.t. criteria set as baselines.

In particular, the WebNLG challenge [3] significantly boosted the proposal of research solutions in NLG, by providing a benchmark corpus of English sentences verbalizing RDF triples. The challenge has been repeated in 2020 [21], including a larger corpus in both English and Russian and adding the subtask of parsing natural language text in RDF. The current dataset refers to 15 categories of resources. The object of the challenge is, again, improving the performance in the generation of baseline sentences rather than proposing forms of verbalization lending to richer explanation.

Traditionally, NLG approaches have been based on rules and templates (see [2], among others), that make such solutions highly domain-dependent and demanding manual intervention.

Recently, the advancements in deep learning have opened the way to neural network-based NLG models. Among them, the Sequence to Sequence (SEQ2SEQ) framework [17] has been employed by Vougiouklis *et al.* [18] to propose a framework, Neural Wikipedian, to generate summaries of RDF triples. The approach is able to summarize triples involving the same entity either as a subject or as an object, but, again, only explicitly stated facts are verbalized and anonymous resources are not managed.

Also the Neural Entity Summarization of Li *et al.* [11] collects only triples that are already present in the RDF descriptions, without handling blank nodes.

Differently from the above approaches, we propose a template-based method that can use blank nodes to abstract several triples with common predicate/object, and, more importantly, can chain triples with blank nodes that eventually reach the same known object (see the example about contracting processes in Sect. 5.1). The informative potential of our method is in the logic-based computation of the RDF graph to verbalize: a rooted graph summarizing in triples the commonalities shared by groups of RDF resources. We show in the rest of the paper how this method for NLG may support the explanation of RDF similarity.

3 LCS in RDF

To make this paper self-contained, we briefly recall here the definition of Least Common Subsumer (LCS) from works by Colucci *et al.* [4,5], along with some preliminary notions. First of all, to compare specific resources r, s in RDF, we need the definition of *rooted* RDF *-graph* (in brief *r-graph*): a pair $\langle r, T_r \rangle$ which isolates resource r inside the RDF-graph T_r. Secondly, $G[s \rightarrow t]$ denotes the graph obtained from G by substituting each occurrence of s with t. Then, the definition of Simple Entailment $T_r \models T_s$ [8] between two RDF-graphs T_r, T_s, is extended to r-graphs as follows [4, Def. 6]:

Definition 1 *[Rooted Entailment]. Let* $\langle r, T_r \rangle, \langle s, T_s \rangle$ *be two r-graphs. We say that* $\langle r, T_r \rangle$ *entails* $\langle s, T_s \rangle$ *—denoted by* $\langle r, T_r \rangle \models \langle s, T_s \rangle$ *—in exactly these cases:*

1. *if s is a blank node, then*
   (a) *if r is not a blank node,* $T_r \models T_s[s \mapsto r]$ *must hold;*
   (b) *if also r is a blank node, then* $T_r[r \mapsto u] \models T_s[s \mapsto u]$ *must hold for a new URI u occurring neither in* T_r *nor in* T_s;
2. *otherwise (i.e., s is not a blank node), if* $s = r$, *then* $T_r \models T_s$ *must hold.*

In all other cases (i.e., s is not a blank node and $s \neq r$), $\langle r, T_r \rangle$ *never entails* $\langle s, T_s \rangle$.

Intuitively, Rooted Entailment extends Simple Entailment with the requirement that the root of a graph is mapped to the root of the other. When both resources r, s are URI, this is possible only when $s = r$ (Case 2), while when either r or s is a blank node (Cases 1b and 1a), the mapping is enforced by a suitable substitution.

Rooted Entailment is at the basis of the definition a Common Subsumer (CS) of two r-graphs $\langle a, T_a \rangle, \langle b, T_b \rangle$:

Definition 2 (Common Subsumer, [4, Def. 7]). *Let* $\langle a, T_a \rangle, \langle b, T_b \rangle$ *be two r-graphs. An r-graph* $\langle x, T_x \rangle$ *is a Common Subsumer (CS) of* $\langle a, T_a \rangle, \langle b, T_b \rangle$ *iff both* $\langle a, T_a \rangle \models \langle x, T_x \rangle$ *and* $\langle b, T_b \rangle \models \langle x, T_x \rangle$.

Finally, a Least Common Subsumer (LCS) of two RDF resources can be defined as follows:

Definition 3 (Least Common Subsumer [4, Def. 8]). *Let* $\langle a, T_a \rangle, \langle b, T_b \rangle$ *be two r-graphs. An r-graph* $\langle x, T_x \rangle$ *is a Least Common Subsumer (LCS) of* $\langle a, T_a \rangle$, $\langle b, T_b \rangle$ *iff both conditions below hold:*

1. $\langle x, T_x \rangle$ *is a CS of* $\langle a, T_a \rangle, \langle b, T_b \rangle$;

2. *for every other CS $\langle y, T_y \rangle$ of $\langle a, T_a \rangle$, $\langle b, T_b \rangle$:*
   if $\langle y, T_y \rangle \models_{\mathcal{R}} \langle x, T_x \rangle$ then $\langle x, T_x \rangle \models_{\mathcal{R}} \langle y, T_y \rangle$, (i.e., $\langle x, T_x \rangle$ and $\langle y, T_y \rangle$ are equivalent under Simple Entailment).

Colucci *et al.* [4] proved that an LCS of two r-graphs is unique—up to blank renaming—so we can talk about "the" LCS. Moreover, the LCS enjoys the following properties:

- Idempotency: $LCS(\langle a, T_a \rangle, \langle a, T_a \rangle) = \langle a, T_a \rangle$
- Commutativity: $LCS(\langle a, T_a \rangle, \langle b, T_b \rangle) = LCS(\langle b, T_b \rangle, \langle a, T_a \rangle)$
- Associativity:
  $LCS(\langle a, T_a \rangle, LCS(\langle b, T_b \rangle, \langle c, T_c \rangle)) = LCS(LCS(\langle a, T_a \rangle, \langle b, T_b \rangle), \langle c, T_c \rangle).$

Associativity relies on a fundamental property of LCSs: the LCS of two r-graphs is itself an r-graph, so it can be used as the argument of another LCS operation with a third r-graph, and so forth. Associativity ensures that the order in which resources are taken—when computing the LCS of all of them—does not matter.

We also recall some definitions modifying the basic notions of Graph Theory to RDF-graphs [4], used in the rest of the paper. First, an RDF-*path* from r to s is a sequence of triples $t_1, \ldots, t_n$ in which the subject of t_1 is r, *either* the predicate *or* the object of t_n is s, and for $i = 1, ..., n-1$, either the predicate or the object of t_i is the subject of t_{i+1}. A resource r is RDF-*connected* to a resource s if there exists an RDF-path from r to s. The *length* of such an RDF-path is n, and the RDF-*distance* between two resources is the length of the shortest RDF-path between them. Also, the RDF-distance between a resource r and a triple t is the shortest RDF-distance between r and the subject of t—in particular, triples which r is the subject of, have zero-RDF-distance from r itself, as expected.

We propose to use the LCS of a cluster of RDF resources—where the cluster can be obtained in any way—to explain their commonalities. To this end, we attached to the construction of an LCS its verbalization in English common language, as described in the next section.

4   From LCS r-Graphs to NLG Explanation

Our approach generates a verbal explanation of the similarity of groups of RDF resources, starting from the triples in their LCS.

Real applications managing RDF resources need some preliminary choices to ensure feasibility. In fact, RDF-based applications cannot take all triples describing a resource r into account, given the huge and always increasing dimensions of available datasets. Thus, it is crucial to select which triples qualify r and build its r-graph. Colucci *et al.* [4] proposed explicit criteria for this choice:

1. data sources: which datasets (one or more) to explore for the comparison;
2. RDF-distance: exclude triples which are "too far" from r;
3. stop-patterns: exclude triples which fit a given pattern $\ll s\ p\ o \gg$;

4. connectedness: there must be an RDF-path from r to the subject of each chosen triple.

Notably, the first three choice criteria can be parameterized for the particular application at hand.

Still, the computed LCS may contain too many triples which, although logically implied by the r-graphs of all analyzed resources, provide little information. Colucci *et al.* name these triples *uninformative triples*, and propose to eliminate them from the comparison result. The result is a—no more Least—Common Subsumer, containing only the most informative triples deducible from all r-graphs.

The set of stop-patterns and uninformative triples used in this paper include both general patterns/triples (to be discarded in every application domain), and some domain-dependent patterns/triples, defined through the analysis of our results.

We propose a template-based NLG tool for explaining the content of a CS we consider significant for the similarity analysis at hand. In fact, the tool allows developers to flexibly set the context of analysis through the specification of the list of uninformative triples, the datasets to explore, the RDF-distance and the stop-patterns to be considered (coherently with the criteria for triples selection recalled above). Such settings tune the practical significance of the CS and, consequently, increase the effectiveness of communication.

We recall that r-graphs modeling CSs include blank nodes by construction (see Definition 1). To the best of our knowledge, no NLG tool is able to verbalize triples involving blank nodes in any position, so this is an original feature of our tool.

The tool works in three steps:

1. it takes as input a set of resources to be compared and application-specific parameters (datasets, RDF-distance, stop-patterns, uninformative triples);
2. it computes the CS parameterized as in Step 1
3. it generates a verbal explanation from the CS computed at Step 2

Step 3 implements a template-based approach, which allows developers to flexibly provide, as application-specific parameters, a dictionary for resources involved in triples, with particular reference to two kinds of undetermined resources: IRIs of involved blank nodes and IRIs of resources not further described in the datasets (even though not modeled as blank nodes).

5   Approach Demonstration

We show how we implemented our explanation approach with two use cases involving aggregation by similarity: the comparison of contracting processes in public procurement in the dataset released with TheyBuyForYou project [15] and the comparison and clustering of drugs in Drugbank [19]. In both cases, we show how to customize the approach w.r.t. the specific knowledge domain, to demonstrate its generality and flexibility.

5.1   Explaining Similarity of Contracting Processes in Public Procurement

The contracting process in procurement includes the procedures followed by a business entity when purchasing services or products: it starts when company managers identify a business need that must be fulfilled and ends when the contract is awarded and signed.

The proposal of easily accessible data-driven solutions supporting (especially public) contracting has been recently addressed. In particular, the Global Public Procurement Database (GPPD)[1] includes a country comparison functionality, that provides to users a side-by-side view of information on countries and regions, helping them to compare country profiles, procurement practices, laws and regulations, and performance indicators.

Also, a specific Contracting Data Comparison (CDC) platform[2] was developed by the Open Contracting Partnership (OCP), an independent non-profit organization born with the aim of publishing and using open, accessible and timely information on public contracting. To the best of our knowledge, none of such solutions is able to automatically compute implicit commonalities, to highlight shared features and explain the similarity of compared resources.

We here show our explanation approach w.r.t. the knowledge graph (in RDF) released with TheyBuyForYou project [15]. The project provides a platform with advanced knowledge-based tools for public procurement, including anomaly detection, cross-lingual document search, and storytelling tool. No tool for resources comparison and its explanation is provided with it.

Our method describes in English common language the commonalities among a set of contracting processes, by first computing their LCS.

TheyBuyForYou knowledge graph includes an ontology for procurement data, based on the Open Contracting Data Standard (OCDS) [16]. The OCDS data model is built around the concept of a contracting process, whose main phases are planning, tender, award, contract, and implementation.

In our example, we compare three RDF resources describing different contracting processes:

1. a public procurement issued by the Gateshead Council[3] for the supply of two lots of two 3.5t flatbed trucks with Tail-lift:
   http://data.tbfy.eu/contractingProcess/ocds-0c46vo-0001-76e76119-992d-40ef-8444-7b020809ff81
2. a tender for trucks supply issued by the Ringkøbing-Skjern municipality[4]:
   http://data.tbfy.eu/contractingProcess/ocds-0c46vo-0133-026258-2019

---

[1] https://www.globalpublicprocurementdata.org/gppd/.
[2] https://www.open-contracting.org/2014/04/30/comparing-contract-data-understanding-supply/.
[3] https://www.gateshead.gov.uk.
[4] https://www.rksk.dk.

3. a public tender for the supply of trucks with multi-lift equipment and three containers issued by the district council of Azuaga[5] http://data.tbfy.eu/contractingProcess/ocds-0c46vo-0203-2019-SUM-1

Recall from Sect. 4 that the approach for computing an LCS in RDF asks for (1) the specification of the RDF-distance to be covered, (2) the list of patterns to ignore (stop-patterns) in the exploration, and (3) the list of triples to be removed in the final result because of their irrelevancy (uninformative triples).

In this example we set an RDF-distance equal to 2 for exploration, showing how a deep exploration of the knowledge graph may lead to significant similarity

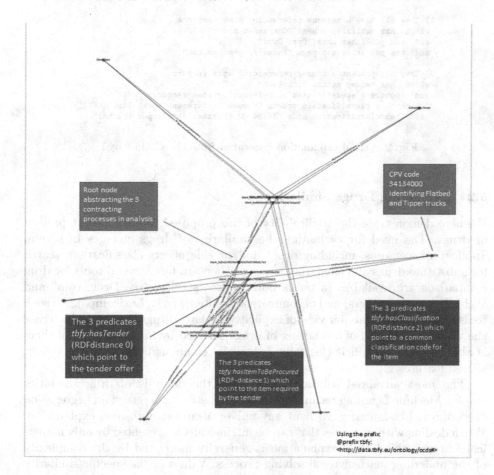

Fig. 1. A CS at RDF-distance 2 between three different contracting processes: i) a public tender for the supply of two flatbed trucks with tail-lift issued by the Gateshead Council; ii) a tender for the supply of trucks issued by the Ringkøbing-Skjern municipality; iii) a tender for the supply of trucks with multi-lift equipment and three containers issued by the district council of Azuaga

---

[5] http://www.azuaga.es.

results. Thus, we first compute a significant CS at RDF-distance 2 of the three resources listed above, w.r.t. a set of stop-patterns and uninformative triples defined through the analysis of our examples. We show this CS in Fig. 1.

Then, we show in Fig. 2 the natural language text generated from the CS in Fig. 1. The reader may observe that the callouts in Fig. 1 correspond to part of the content in description item 2) in Fig. 2. In particular, the callouts show the full path (RDF-distance 2) from the CS root to the classification code "34134000".

```
The resources in analysis present the following properties in common:

1) They all have a release referencing some resource
which  has publisher schema "Companies House"
and  has publisher name "Open Opps"
and  has publisher web page "https://openopps.com"

2) They all present a tender referencing some resource
which  has tender status "complete"
and  require a specific item(s) referencing some resource
  which  has classification schema "Common Procurement Vocabulary (CPV)"
  and  has classification code "34134000 (Flatbed and Tipper trucks)"
```

Fig. 2. Verbal explanation generated from the CS in Fig. 1.

5.2 Explaining Drugs Similarity

We here demonstrate the applicability of the proposed tool to the comparison of drugs. The need for evaluating the similarity of drugs emerges in several application scenarios, including drugs and/or side effects classification, search for substitute drugs and clustering, among others. In fact, several tools for drug comparison are available, in terms both of free services (see Drugs.com[6] and WebMD[7], among others) and of commercial solutions (*e.g.*, Lexicomp[8]). All such tools offer a parallel tabular view of explicitly declared drugs features, which ease the visual comparison of a small set of drugs selected by the user. None of them is able to extract implicit (logically deducible) commonalities and to highlight shared features.

The most advanced solutions addressing the analysis of drug similarity employ Machine Learning techniques based on metrics and return an aggregation of resources by similarity, without any universal and easy-to-read explanation. When dealing with resources that can be intrinsically represented by only numerical features, this lack of explanation is generally motivated by the complexity of the underling mathematical solving process. Values of the specific similarity

---

[6] https://www.drugs.com/compare/.

[7] https://www.webmd.com/drugs/compare.

[8] https://www.wolterskluwer.com/en/solutions/lexicomp/resources/facts-comparisons-user-academy/drug-comparisons.

measure represent the reason why resources are aggregated, as the only source of explanation.

Instead, when resources are described in formal languages endowed with semantics, like RDF, more informative and logic-based forms of explanation may be returned. Our method describes in English common language the commonalities among a set of drugs defined in RDF, by first computing their LCS.

We first show such a human-readable explanation for the similarity of a pair of resources manually selected from Drugbank[9]: Amphetamine (drugbank:DB00182) and Phentermine (drugbank:DB00191), with the following prefix:

@prefix drugbank: <https://bio2rdf.org/drugbank>.

Our example refers to two values of RDF-distance, 0 and 1, to show the impact on final explanation of a deeper exploration of the information source. Stop-patterns and uninformative triples have been set according to heuristics evaluated in the performance of our examples.

Figure 3 shows a screenshot of our tool. The upper part includes the set of triples describing a significant CS of the analyzed pair of r-graphs when the RDF-distance of their triples is set to 0 (*i.e.*, only triples whose subject is the resource itself are included in the r-graph). Lower part of Fig. 3 shows the explanation generated by the tool, starting from the triples in the upper part.

Fig. 3. A screenshot of the tool generating an explanation (lower window) for the RDF triples in a CS at RDF-distance 0 of a resources set (upper window).

---

[9] https://old.datahub.io/dataset/fu-berlin-drugbank.

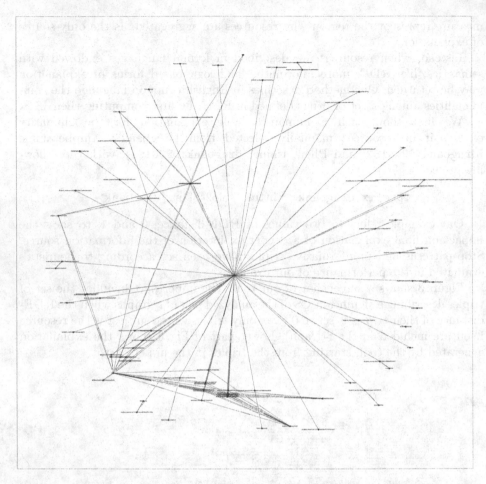

Fig. 4. A CS between Amphetamine (`drugbank:DB00182`) and Phentermine (`drugbank:DB00191`), computed from r-graphs including only triples at RDF-distance 1 from each resource). The figure is meant to give an idea of the complexity of the CS structure, without delving into details about involved resources. Note that this representation of the commonalities of the two resources, although pictorial, is still ineffective as an explanation.

Figure 4 shows a CS graph at RDF-distance 1 of the analyzed pair.

In Fig. 5, we show only the verbalization of triples added when passing from r-graphs with triples at RDF-distance 0 to r-graphs including also triples at RDF-distance 1. The complete explanation of the CS depicted in Fig. 4 could be obtained by combining Figs. 3(lower part) and 5.

As the reader may observe, the number of triples collected in the CS at RDF-distance 1 is significantly high, but some of them may be considered uninformative, according to our analysis. In particular, in addition to the triples originally put in the set of uninformative triples (and then not returned in the

```
The resources in analysis present the following properties in common:

1) They share the property "target" each one of them referencing some resource
   which has organism type "Human"
   and  has cellular location "Membrane, multi-pass membrane protein"

2) They share the property "mechanism of effecting the body" each one of them referencing some resource
   which has semantic type  "Mechanism of action"

3) They share the property "enzyme" each one of them referencing some resource
   which has organism type "Human"
   and has transmembrane regions of effect: "None"
   and has cellular location  "Endoplasmic reticulum"

6) They share the property "toxicity" each one of them referencing some  resource
   which  has semantic type "toxicity"
```

Fig. 5. Verbal explanation generated from the CS in Fig. 4; we show only the verbal explanation of paths in the CS leading to triples at RDF-distance 1.

graph in Fig. 4), we excluded from the explanation also triples including URI not further described nor labeled in Drugbank.

We notice that our approach is able to generate a verbal explanation also from triples involving blank nodes, which are crucial in the computation of the LCS to abstract the commonalities of different resources at every RDF-distance form the root. To the best of our knowledge, such an ability is not available in any developed NLG tool. The informative potential of blank nodes treatment in our tool may be evaluated by looking at the content of Fig. 5: all the sentences not in the first row of each figure item contain a relative sentence—starting with the relative pronoun "which"—that refers to "some resource" (an undetermined object represented by a blank node).

From now on, we show our explanation results, referring to a group of RDF resources aggregated by similarity thorough standard methods, with a twofold aim: *(i)* considering items supposed to be similar in an agnostic fashion, without manually selecting them; *(ii)* showing the behaviour of the explanation approach over groups of resources rather than pairs.

To this aim, we show the explanation of the commonalities shared by clusters of drugs returned by a standard clustering algorithm applied on Drugbank. In particular, we applied the k-means algorithm in the Scikit-learn[10] Python library setting the number of clusters and the maximum number of iterations parameters equal to 125 and 400, respectively (such settings result from a standard validation process).

Figure 6 shows the explanation corresponding to the LCS (at RDF-distance 0) of all the 13 items returned in one of the clusters returned by the k-means implementation described above. The cluster included the following drugs:

Notably, the computed LCS is almost completely uninformative because it includes really generic features shared by items in the cluster. Apparently, the aggregation returned by k-means, that is purely numeric, does not reflect the logical content of analyzed resources. This behaviour suggests a possible

---

[10] https://scikit-learn.org/stable/modules/generated/sklearn.cluster.KMeans.html.

```
Cathinone [drugbank:DB01560]          Aprindine [drugbank:DB01429]
Etidronic acid [drugbank:DB01077]     Metocurine [drugbank:DB01336]
Papaverine [drugbank:DB01113]         Methsuximide [drugbank:DB05246]
Ceftizoxime [drugbank:DB01332]        Pentosan Polysulfate [drugbank:DB00686]
Tipranavir [drugbank:DB00932]         Atomoxetine [drugbank:DB00289]
Clonazepam [drugbank:DB01068]         Paclitaxel [drugbank:DB01229]
Pentobarbital [drugbank:DB00312]
```

```
The resources in analysis present the following properties in common:

1) Their type is "small molecule"
2) They share the property "kingdom",
   all of them referencing the same resource not further described in the dataset
```

Fig. 6. Verbal explanation generated from the LCS at RDF-distance 0 of a cluster of RDF resources returned by k-means. Note that the common content has very little relevance for explanation.

byproduct of our tool: the produced explanation may be used as a fast-checker for the significance of results in the fine tuning of tools for clustering resources modeled in RDF.

6   Conclusion

We presented a logic-based methodology and a tool for the explanation of the similarities of a group of RDF resources, which can be pipelined to any Data-driven similarity aggregation tool, including Business Intelligence ones. Our methodology is agnostic w.r.t. the aggregation criterion and produces a verbal explanation of commonalities among groups of resources which the aggregation tool found to be similar.

Our tool works in two steps: first, the LCS of the analyzed set of resources is computed, as an abstraction of commonalities in the form of RDF triples; then, the LCS is translated into a verbal explanation, communicating only the effective knowledge. We presented the explanations given by our tool in two different use cases: Public Procurement and Drug comparison. Our methodology is domain-independent and can be adapted to several contexts (we omitted a third use case about Twitter accounts for lack of space). Also the significance of returned explanation may be tuned through the specification of patterns uninformative for the analyzed context.

Thus, our approach is potentially able to explain the similarity of RDF resources in every scenario, with a flexible level of communication effectiveness. The informative potential of our explanation is double-tied to the logic-based nature of the underlying theory, showing that the synergy between numerical and logical methods may improve explainability of Data-driven tools.

Acknowledgements. Projects Regione Lazio-DTC/"SanLo" (CUP F85F21001090 003) and MISE (FSC 2014–2020)/"BARIUM5G" (CUP D94I20000160002) partially supported this work.

References

1. Bouayad-Agha, N., Casamayor, G., Wanner, L.: Natural language generation in the context of the semantic web. Semant. Web **5**(6), 493–513 (2014)
2. Cimiano, P., Lüker, J., Nagel, D., Unger, C.: Exploiting ontology lexica for generating natural language texts from RDF data. In: Proceedings of the 14th European Workshop on Natural Language Generation, Sofia, Bulgaria, pp. 10–19. Association for Computational Linguistics, August 2013. https://aclanthology.org/W13-2102
3. Colin, E., Gardent, C., M'rabet, Y., Narayan, S., Perez-Beltrachini, L.: The webNLG challenge: generating text from DBpedia data. In: Proceedings of the 9th International Natural Language Generation Conference, pp. 163–167 (2016)
4. Colucci, S., Donini, F., Giannini, S., Di Sciascio, E.: Defining and computing least common subsumers in RDF. Web Semant. Sci. Serv. Agents World Wide Web **39**, 62–80 (2016)
5. Colucci, S., Donini, F.M., Di Sciascio, E.: Common subsumbers in RDF. In: Baldoni, M., Baroglio, C., Boella, G., Micalizio, R. (eds.) AI*IA 2013. LNCS (LNAI), vol. 8249, pp. 348–359. Springer, Cham (2013). https://doi.org/10.1007/978-3-319-03524-6_30
6. Colucci, S., Giannini, S., Donini, F.M., Di Sciascio, E.: A deductive approach to the identification and description of clusters in linked open data. In: Proceedings of the 21st European Conference on Artificial Intelligence (ECAI 2014). IOS Press (2014)
7. Ghosal, A., Nandy, A., Das, A.K., Goswami, S., Panday, M.: A short review on different clustering techniques and their applications. In: Mandal, J.K., Bhattacharya, D. (eds.) Emerging Technology in Modelling and Graphics. AISC, vol. 937, pp. 69–83. Springer, Singapore (2020). https://doi.org/10.1007/978-981-13-7403-6_9
8. Hayes, P., Patel-Schneider, P.F.: RDF 1.1 semantics, W3C recommendation (2014). www.w3.org/TR/2014/REC-rdf11-mt-20140225/
9. Huang, L., Luo, H., Li, S., Wu, F.X., Wang, J.: Drug-drug similarity measure and its applications. Briefings Bioinform. **22**(4) (2020)
10. Li, J., Zhang, Y., Qian, C., Ma, S., Zhang, G.: Research on recommendation and interaction strategies based on resource similarity in the manufacturing ecosystem. Adv. Eng. Inform. **46**, 101183 (2020). www.sciencedirect.com/science/article/pii/S1474034620301543
11. Li, J., et al.: Neural entity summarization with joint encoding and weak supervision. In: Bessiere, C. (ed.) Proceedings of IJCAI-2020, pp. 1644–1650. ijcai.org (2020). https://doi.org/10.24963/ijcai.2020/228
12. Michalski, R.S.: Knowledge acquisition through conceptual clustering: a theoretical framework and an algorithm for partitioning data into conjunctive concepts. Int. J. Policy Anal. Inf. Syst. **4**, 219–244 (1980)
13. Pérez-Suárez, A., Martínez-Trinidad, J.F., Carrasco-Ochoa, J.A.: A review of conceptual clustering algorithms. Artif. Intell. Rev. **52**(2), 1267–1296 (2019). https://doi.org/10.1007/s10462-018-9627-1
14. Saxena, A., et al.: A review of clustering techniques and developments. Neurocomputing **267**, 664–681 (2017)

15. Soylu, A., et al.: TheyBuyForYou platform and knowledge graph: expanding horizons in public procurement with open linked data. Semant. Web **13**(2), 265–291 (2022)
16. Soylu, A., et al.: Towards an ontology for public procurement based on the open contracting data standard. In: Pappas, I.O., Mikalef, P., Dwivedi, Y.K., Jaccheri, L., Krogstie, J., Mäntymäki, M. (eds.) I3E 2019. LNCS, vol. 11701, pp. 230–237. Springer, Cham (2019). https://doi.org/10.1007/978-3-030-29374-1_19
17. Sutskever, I., Vinyals, O., Le, Q.V.: Sequence to sequence learning with neural networks. In: Proceedings of the 27th International Conference on Neural Information Processing Systems, NIPS 2014, vol. 2, pp. 3104–3112, Cambridge, MA, USA. MIT Press (2014)
18. Vougiouklis, P., et al.: Neural Wikipedian: generating textual summaries from knowledge base triples. J. Web Semant. **52–53**, 1–15 (2018). www.sciencedirect.com/science/article/pii/S1570826818300313
19. Wishart, D.S., et al.: DrugBank: a knowledgebase for drugs, drug actions and drug targets. Nucleic Acids Res. **36**(suppl 1), D901–D906 (2008)
20. Yu, Y., Umashankar, N., Rao, V.R.: Choosing the right target: relative preferences for resource similarity and complementarity in acquisition choice. Strat. Manag. J. **37**(8), 1808–1825 (2016). https://onlinelibrary.wiley.com/doi/abs/10.1002/smj.2416
21. Zhou, G., Lampouras, G.: WebNLG challenge 2020: language agnostic delexicalisation for multilingual RDF-to-text generation. In: Proceedings of the 3rd International Workshop on Natural Language Generation from the Semantic Web (WebNLG+), Dublin, Ireland (Virtual), pp. 186–191. Association for Computational Linguistics, December 2020. https://aclanthology.org/2020.webnlg-1.22

Analysis of Data Center Development Problems in the Era of Digital Transformation

Andrew V. Toutov, Natalia V. Toutova(✉), and Anatoly S. Vorozhtsov

Moscow Technical University of Communication and Informatics, Moscow, Russia
e-natasha@mail.ru

Abstract. The main problems of the development of telecom operators and cloud service providers are analyzed. In response to modern challenges, such as the unprecedented growth in the use of digital services in the world, the Internet of Things, which fosters the emergence of big data and the introduction of machine learning, telecom operators and service providers are faced with the task of improving their own IT infrastructure to quickly respond to the growing needs of society. In addition, the large-scale digital transformation announced by the government of the Russian Federation, focused on the implementation of domestic solutions, creates new challenges for data centers. The main cycle of works on the management of computing resources of cloud data centers is proposed, which are based on a set of models and methods for the optimal allocation of computing resources.

Keywords: Data centers · Optimization · VM placement · Resource allocation

1 Introduction

Data centers play a critical role in digital transformation projects that are carried out in the world. In November 2021 Prime Minister of Russian Federation Mikhail Mishustin announced a large-scale digital transformation in industry. In social sphere the program of digital transformation was already approved. All these projects are being implemented within the framework of the national project "Digital Economy of the Russian Federation". The program indicates the need to develop systems based on domestic software.

Modern data centers are very different than they were just a short time ago. Infrastructure has shifted from traditional on-premises physical servers to virtual networks that support applications and workloads across pools of physical infrastructure and into a multicloud environment. Digital transformation is challenging data centers. In this paper, the main problems and challenges are discussed. The main cycle of works on the management of computing resources of cloud data centers is proposed, which are based on a set of models and methods for the optimal allocation of computing resources.

E. Babkin et al. (Eds.): MOBA 2022, LNBIP 457, pp. 65–72, 2022.
https://doi.org/10.1007/978-3-031-17728-6_6

2   The Main Problems and Challenges

2.1   Global Growth in Traffic

The first challenge is the global growth in traffic. Analysts form IDC predict 175 ZB of data globally by 2025 [1]. This data will need to not only be stored, but also processed. The latest events with pandemic have resulted in increased volumes of data generated from various sources, such as working employees from home. The demand for cloud applications dramatically has grown. For example, Zoom reached more than 200 million daily meetings participants, a dramastic increase over its previos record of 10 million. Cloud and content delivery service provider Akamai reported a 50% increase in internet traffic compared to average [2]. The cloud computing environment is a actual hero in the COVID crisis. We need data centers more than ever to support the increased demand for stable online services.

2.2   Internet of Things, Big Data and Machine Learning

The generation of streaming data from the Internet of Things (IoT) sensors and cyber-physical systems are deployed. The amount of such data will grow many times over and could exceed the amount of data available on the public WWW, in enterprises and in mobile clouds [3].

Some IoT and smart city applications require feedback, such as video from millions of city surveillance cameras, self-driving cars and drones. This makes the latency and bandwidth between the network edge and the cloud a significant limitation for performing analytics. Therefore, edge or fog computing has emerged and is beginning to complement cloud computing on edge devices [4].

The need to process the "big data" generated in recent years and the increase in computing power have led to the development of the field of artificial intelligence. New machine learning models and algorithms are being developed in various applications. A cloud data center is a platform for hosting machine learning services. In addition, machine learning is used to more efficiently use cloud services and the infrastructure of the data centers themselves. Many cloud services have auto-tuning functions, for example, simplifying the selection of cloud instances or optimizing the selection of resources.

One of the difficult and current research areas is the creation of reusable machine learning models that can be used by multiple users in different contexts instead of creating multiple solutions from scratch [3].

2.3   Multi-cloud Environments

Cloud service providers and platforms are fragmented. Therefore, the interaction of clouds remains an open problem. Mechanisms are needed to share computing, storage and network resources of different clouds. Cloud interoperability should be seen as the ability of public clouds, private clouds and other heterogeneous systems to "understand" system interfaces, configurations, forms of authentication and authorization, data formats, initialization procedures and application configuration [5].

In general, approaches can be classified as federated cloud computing if the connection is initiated and managed by the special provider such as InterCloud, or hybrid clouds if created and managed by users or a third party on behalf of users.

2.4 Reliability and Security

There is an urgent need for new ways of delivering cloud services with guaranteed performance and resilience to deal with all types of independent and correlated failures.

Security is also a major concern in ICT systems, and cloud computing is not exception. There is an annual increase in hacker attacks. In Russia, the number of cyberattacks increases by about 20% last years [6].

2.5 Power Consumption

The major problem remains power consumption. Data centers consume colossal amounts of electricity, more than the entire aviation industry [7]. Data center infrastructure must be built to cope with potential peaks that rarely occur in practice. This leads to insufficient utilization of some of the data center resources. Rapid improvements in energy efficiency have, however, helped limit energy demand growth from data centres and data transmission networks, which each account for about 1% of global electricity use. Nevertheless, strong government and industry efforts on energy efficiency will be essential to curb energy demand and emissions growth over the next decade.

The main consumers of electricity in the data center are the infocommunication system, consisting of computing, telecommunications and data storage subsystems, as well as engineering systems. The cooling system the cooling subsystem consumes up to 40% of all electricity [7]. The cooling system starts working hard in case of uneven temperature distribution and additionally consumes electricity. Thus, in order to increase the energy efficiency of the data center, it is necessary to consider the work of subsystems comprehensively.

Idle servers need to be powered off or hibernated, as the cost of excess capacity is significant and includes the cost of additional capacity for cooling, power distribution, generators, uninterruptible power supplies, and so on.

2.6 Scaling, Elasticity and Quality of Service

All advantages of cloud computing can only be realized if the infrastructure supports scalable services and resources, as well as the ability to dynamically add and remove resources depending on the load, the so-called resource elasticity.

Virtualization makes it possible to flexibly scale virtual machine resources to meet the needs of applications. One of the most important research tasks related to elastic services is the ability to accurately predict computational needs and application performance under various resource allocation schemes, using workload models when making resource management decisions [3].

3   Related Works

In order to cope with the described challenges, it is necessary to increase the efficiency of resource management of the infocommunication system of data centers.

To date, there is a large number of works devoted to individual tasks of managing cloud data center resources to maintain the stability and performance of cloud services. Much attention is paid to the placement of virtual machines (VM) on physical servers. We consider the tasks of static and dynamic placement, which is carried out by migrating VMs between servers, taking into account the current load of resources. For example, [8] describes two resource management software products used in conjunction with ESX hypervisors from VMware. In the first product, Distributed Resource Scheduler (DRS), VM migrations provide load balancing across a cluster of physical hosts. A second Distributed Power Management (DPM) solution expands DRS capabilities by reducing the number of hosts and thereby reducing power consumption. In the Mail.ru Cloud Solutions cloud, the developers have implemented their own version of the DRS implementation [9].

However, these systems use simple heuristics that do not provide an optimal solution. To maintain the stability and quality of cloud services, the best option would be to develop a system that allows at each stage of the main work cycle to find an optimal solution, taking into account several conflicting criteria, such as power consumption, heat dissipation, violation of SLA agreements and the minimum remaining unused resources. The proposed main cycle of work is based on models and methods of multicriteria optimization of the resources of the data center infocommunication system to obtain the most effective indicators of its functioning.

4   The Main Cycle of Work on Data Center Resource Management

The typical architecture of a cloud data center resource management system is two-tier, consisting of local and global controllers. A local controller is located on each physical server and is a virtual machine (VM) monitor module. Its task is to constantly monitor the load and temperature of the processor and transfer data to the central storage of the global controller. The Global Controller analyzes this information and, according to it, makes decisions about migration of virtual machines.

The main cycle of work on cloud data center resource management consists of the following stages:

- VM sizing, scaling;
- VM placement;
- resource and temperature monitoring;
- dynamic resource allocation though live migration.

At the first stage, the number of virtual machines and their sizes are determined, which are set by users, or are determined automatically using the models and methods of autoscaling at the SaaS and PaaS levels discussed in [10, 11]. The second stage is the placement of the VM. To do this, the problem of the initial placement of the VM is solved, taking into account the criteria for power consumption, server temperature, violation of SLA agreements and uniform resource load. This problem is considered in works [11, 12]. The stages of solving the problem of initial placement are shown in Fig. 1.

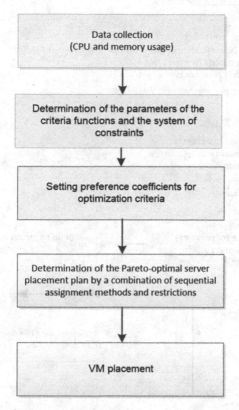

Fig. 1. Stages of static placement of virtual machines.

Monitoring and forecasting the load and temperature of the processors of physical servers is a continuous step carried out by the local controllers of the resource management system. To ensure the stability of the system, observation is carried out using the sliding window method, the optimal size of which is selected depending on the duration of the VM migration. The initial size of the sliding window, when statistics has not yet been accumulated, it is recommended to choose in the range of 3–5 min to load the processor and 4–6 min to monitor the temperature. In order for VM migrations not to interfere with the process of monitoring servers, the size of the observation window should be larger than the duration of the migration, optimally 3 times [13]. The probability of VM migration duration is determined on the basis of accumulated statistics and is calculated based on the method proposed in [14, 15]. The best forecasting results based on the results of the research described in [11] are given by the method of group data handling (GMDH). The processor load and temperature of each physical server is predicted, and when an overload or underload is detected, a decision is made to migrate virtual machines. The stages of dynamic placement are shown in Fig. 2.

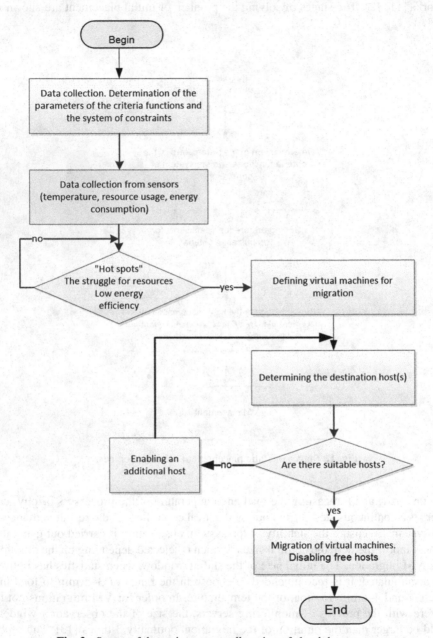

Fig. 2. Stages of dynamic resource allocation of cloud data centers.

In case of server overload, one VM is selected, and in case of underload, all VMs are selected for migration to other servers. To determine new destination servers for the selected virtual machines, the task of optimizing the placement of VMs is solved according to the criteria of the minimum combined criterion for violations of SLA agreements and uneven resource utilization. The statement of the problem and the method for its solution are described in [16]. Simulation has shown that the proposed virtual machine placement method provides 3.5 times better results on the combined ESV metric (power consumption and SLA violations) than the FFD heuristic algorithm, which is widely used in practice, "first fit in descending order".

Thus, the main cycle of work has been developed to optimize and manage the resources of the infocommunication system of data centers, which includes models and methods for the initial and dynamic placement of virtual machines, as well as horizontal scaling, which allows to reduce energy consumption, to meet the requirements of cloud services for the specified in the SLA- quality level agreements and ensure the stability of cloud services.

The presented set of stages of computational work with the developed models and algorithms, designed in the form of a cycle, is sufficient to achieve the set goals of increasing the efficiency of resource management of cloud services, and the cycle can be called the main one. However, it does not take into account one more circumstance, which is that at the moment of making a decision to continue work, one of the stages, in particular the first one, can be skipped as satisfying all the conditions, which makes the moment of starting the work cycle random. This circumstance can be considered using VR/AR methods and technologies, which make it possible to visually represent the process of placing virtual machines in space and time, which is equivalent, for example, to the process of controlling the assembly line of cars, which is well described in the literature. Considering the above circumstance will make the developed mathematical models and algorithms more adequate to real processes.

5 Conclusions

In response to modern challenges, such as the unprecedented growth in the use of digital services in the world, the Internet of Things, which fosters the emergence of big data and the introduction of machine learning, telecom operators and service providers are faced with the task of improving their own IT infrastructure to quickly respond to the growing needs of society.

In addition, the large-scale digital transformation announced by the government of the Russian Federation, focused on the implementation of domestic solutions, creates new challenges for data centers.

The main cycle of work has been developed to optimize and manage the resources of the infocommunication system of data centers, which includes models and methods for the initial and dynamic placement of virtual machines, as well as horizontal scaling, which allows to reduce energy consumption, to meet the requirements of cloud services for the specified in the SLA- quality level agreements and ensure the stability of cloud services.

References

1. Reinsel, D., Gantz, J., Rydning, J.: IDC white paper: Data Age 2025: The Evolution of Data to Life-Critical (2017)
2. COVID-19's Impact on Data Centers. http://ftp.sunbirddcim.com/blog/covid-19-impact-data-centers. Accessed 24 Dec 2021
3. Buyya, R., et al.: A manifesto for future generation cloud computing: research directions for the next decade. ACM Comput. Surv. (CSUR) **51**(5), 1–38 (2018)
4. Mahmud, R., Kotagiri, R., Buyya, R.: Fog computing: a taxonomy, survey and future directions. In: Di Martino, B., Li, K.-C., Yang, L.T., Esposito, A. (eds.) Internet of everything. IT, pp. 103–130. Springer, Singapore (2018). https://doi.org/10.1007/978-981-10-5861-5_5
5. Sotomayor, B., Montero, R.S., Llorente, I.M., Foster, I.: Virtual infrastructure management in private and hybrid clouds. IEEE Internet Comput. **13**(5), 14–22 (2009)
6. Cybersecurity_threatscape-2019. https://www.ptsecurity.com/upload/corporate/ru-ru/analytics/cybersecurity-threatscape-2019-rus.pdf. Accessed 24 Dec 2021
7. How Much Energy Do Data Centers Really Use? https://energyinnovation.org/2020/03/17/how-much-energy-do-data-centers-really-use/. Accessed 24 Dec 2021
8. Gulati, A., Holler, A., Ji, M., Shanmuganathan, G., Waldspurger, C., Zhu, X.: VMware distributed resource management: design, implementation, and lessons learned. VMware Techn. J. **1**(1), 45–64 (2012)
9. DRS as a means of optimizing the placement of virtual machines in the Mail.ru Cloud Solutions cloud. https://habr.com/ru/company/vk/blog/565528/. Accessed 14 Nov 2021
10. Vorozhtsov, A.S., Tutova, N.V., Tutov, A.V.: Performance evaluation of cloud data centers. T-Comm. **8**(5), 69–71 (2014). (in Russian)
11. Tutov, A.V.: Models and methods of resources allocation of infocommunication system in cloud data centers. H&ES Res. **10**(6), 100–200 (2018)
12. Vorozhtsov, A.S., Tutova, N.V., Tutov, A.V.: Optimal cloud servers placement in data centers. T-Comm. **9**(6), 4–8 (2015). (in Russian)
13. Vorozhtsov, A.S., Toutova, N.V., Toutov, A.V.: Resource control system stability of mobile data centers. In: 2018 Systems of Signals Generating and Processing in the Field of on Board Communications, pp. 1–4, IEEE, March 2018
14. Toutov, A.V., Vorozhtsov, A.S., Toutova, N.V.: Estimation of total migration time of virtual machines in cloud data centers. In: 2018 IEEE International Conference Quality Management, Transport and Information Security, Information Technologies (IT&QM&IS), pp. 389–393. IEEE, September 2018
15. Toutov, A., Vorozhtsov, A., Toutova, N.: Analytical approach to estimating total migration time of virtual machines with various applications. Int. J. Embed. Real-Time Commun. Syst. (IJERTCS) **11**(2), 58–75 (2020)
16. Toutov, A., Toutova, N., Vorozhtsov, A., Andreev, I.: Multicriteria optimization of virtual machine placement in cloud data centers. In: 2021 28th Conference of Open Innovations Association (FRUCT), pp. 482–487. IEEE, January 2021

A Theoretical Model for Defining Prerequisites of the IT-Business Alignment in the Social Dimension

Roman Khlebnikov and Pavel Malyzhenkov[✉]

Department of Information Systems and Technologies, National Research University – Higher School of Economics, Bol. Pecherskaya 25, 603155 Nizhny Novgorod, Russia
pmalyzhenkov@hse.ru

Abstract. The role of effective communication between IT and business cannot be overestimated, especially in an era when long-term plans cannot be built. The need for IT and business to consider each other's opinions, to try to build a competent strategy leads to the fact that the social dimension of IT and business alignment is acute for management. This paper describes techniques that allow managers to find ways to realize a mechanism of a consistent IT-business alignment enterprise architecture creation. In this paper a proposal to do it by means of nomological networks tool is presented.

Keywords: IT-business alignment · Social dimension · Nomological networks

1 Introduction

Many CIOs [18] struggle to resist the pressure of new, hyped technologies. They need to innovate in an ever-changing business landscape. The business wants IT to correctly define strategies that can save investments:

1. Need to maintain a balance between long-term strategic goals and new market opportunities
2. Balance between internal and external customer requests

Aligning IT and business is what can help achieve technological and business success. Analysts [19] believe that with changing business goals, IT departments must have the competencies to quickly respond to create and support new solutions. Therefore, the consequence of IT business alignment is the convergence of corporate and consumer technologies. Since in conditions of remote work, business employees should not feel the gap between work and home.

IT-business alignment is still in the top 2 management problems and this picture has not changed for 3 years [20] (Fig. 1).

The aim of the work is to present a theoretical model for the analysis of alignment paths. As well as the opportunity to analyze the prerequisites for the emergence of a common language between IT and business.

E. Babkin et al. (Eds.): MOBA 2022, LNBIP 457, pp. 73–83, 2022.
https://doi.org/10.1007/978-3-031-17728-6_7

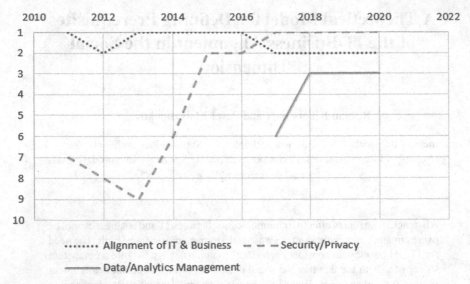

Fig. 1. Alignment as a management issue

Further, the study is structured as follows. Section 2 summarizes the literature analy-sis on this topic. Section 3 presents the apparatus of nomological networks, its structure and composition, its possible application to the IT-business misalignment factors search and the defining of the management actions aimed to establish IT-business alignment. Section 4 summarizes the main findings and directions for future research.

2   Theoretical Review

2.1   Approaches to IT-Business Alignment Analysis

In one of the most widely cited works [10], the author answers the questions why IT-business alignment is so popular among the academic and business communities. Based on earlier work on the creation of strategic planning and IT-business alignment, the author argues that assessing the maturity of alignment is one of the main tasks of managers, because the dependence of harmony between IT and business has been proven and documented since the late 1970s. in works [8]. The author suggests 6 categories of alignment of information systems and business:

1. Communication maturity
Communication between business and IT helps stakeholders to understand joint plans, strategies, risks. Misunderstanding of the business by the IT sector or underestima-tion of the business part of IT potentially deprives the enterprise of an opportunity for investment. This social interaction, according to the author, contains opportunities for growth.

2. Maturity of competency assessment

To demonstrate its usefulness, the IT world must show/develop those metrics that are understandable to the business, and qualitatively and quantitatively capable of influencing decisions. In this way, consistency in performance measures helps the business look at their ideas analytically, and IT demonstrates its contribution to the overall enterprise.

3. Managerial maturity

Luftman [12, 13] singles out a separate block "management in IT", which determines joint business strategies, allocates resources in IT, and controls activities. IT management contributes to alignment by linking business strategies to current capabilities, IT priorities.

4. Maturity of the partnership

In terms of alignment, partnerships are essential in a cross-functional relationship where IT and business are moving towards the same goal but in different ways. As part of partnership maturity, the author believes that management should pay special attention to this component in the face of growing risks.

5. Technological maturity

Flexible, scalable architecture in the face of constant business growth, new technologies - this is what should affect business processes. Because of this, IT business consistency allows IT services to be better deployed to capture returns of scale.

6. Maturity of skills

Luftman [12] cites research that shows that consistency in human resource management and skills can contribute positively to communication and partnerships. The maturity of skills and human resources is an understanding of the need for learning, a willingness to change, and the ability to use new ideas.

Each category has its own set of IT-business mismatch symptoms. Their number shows that this area was and remains dynamic, and the survey tool put forward by the author as an opportunity to assess the level of consistency between business and IT in a particular enterprise, which, in turn, will make it possible to qualitatively manage the business strategy of the enterprise.

In a more recent work [13], Luftman continues the study of SAM (Strategic Alignment Maturity) - a model, suggesting that parts of this model improve the consistency of IT and business. To evaluate the desired impact on alignment, the author proposes to introduce hypotheses, each of which is statistically examined using a model that can be formulated using the hypothesis that IT business alignment, which is expressed in maturity between these six categories of alignment, has a positive effect on the efficiency of the enterprises under study, however, individually, each of them does not have the desired, positive impact. The conclusions demonstrated in the results of the work showed the statistical significance of the hypotheses that the consistency.

2.2 Social Dimension of IT-Business Alignment Problem

The authors of [5] highlight two dimensions of IT-business alignment:

1. Intellectual, based on formally defined facts, methodologies, technologies, as well as information structures in the organization.

2. The social dimension concerns goals, business strategy formulations, communication methods, decision-making methods (Table 1).

Table 1. Dimensions of IT-business alignment

Dimension	Reasons/factors	Effect/link
Intellectual	Methodologies and activities for formulating the IT business mission	The extent to which IT business plans are aligned internally and externally
Social	Exchange of information, participants who take part in the creation of IT business missions	The level of business understanding of the IT mission and vice versa

In their work [5], the authors, as an analyzed hypothesis, assume that 2 sources of assessing the level of social level of consistency between IT and business are determined:

1. Understanding and thinking of managers about the contributions of IT and business;
2. Business/IT artifacts.

Also, 2 time periods are defined as links between the social dimension of IT-business alignment.

In [5], the authors continue their study of factors that influence and/or are sources of the social dimension of IT-Business Alignment. Using a data source to analyze his hypotheses: 10 business units in the life insurance industry, he came to the conclusions:

1. The level of communication between IT and business planning does not affect the overall level of long-term IT business alignment since formal planning does not lead to the creation of an IT vision;
2. The level of mutual participation in each other's processes of IT managers and business managers has little effect on the level of communication between them;
3. The level of communication between IT and business has an impact on the overall level of short-term agreement but has not shown an impact on the long-term.

The work [15] expands on the notion of strategic IT-Business alignment and critically analyzes past work on the topic, for example:

1. Is there a causal relationship between the social and intellectual dimensions of IT business alignment?
2. Is the social dimension or common understanding between IT and business a prerequisite for intellectual alignment or can this dimension be separated into a separate dimension?
3. Is it possible to test empirically the key premises of the social dimension of alignment?

These questions served as the basis for the theoretical development of the author - a research model, which is a nomological network. This model is structured in such a way that "the general understanding as a concept that is described in previous works is a complex structure with its own premises". The author suggests that these prerequisites are factors that can help develop "common understanding" and integration between IT and business managers. In this model, there are 4 main prerequisites for a common understanding [15]:

1. Common language is the level of communication where IT and business use common terminology;
2. Knowledge that is shared between IT and business. For example, the IT manager's knowledge of business strategy, as well as the strategic knowledge of the IT business manager;
3. Knowledge systems;
4. Relative similarities, such as demographics.

Using these prerequisites, the author puts the appropriate hypotheses, which are the theoretical support for conceptual connections. The conclusions made in the framework of this work served as the basis for future research by various authors:

1. The social dimension (general understanding, within the framework of this article) is one of the prerequisites for the intellectual dimension of alignment.
2. Shared understanding is a framework of common language, business knowledge of IT managers, and top management's strategic vision
3. The sharing of knowledge systems as well as the organization of educational events are important variables that influence the overall strategic impact between IT and business.

For example, the article [16], while continuing to address the social dimension of IT-Business alignment, also uses a survey tool to find alignment paths, but deviates from the strategic level explored by previous authors. Therefore, the proposed hypotheses really expand the understanding of the social dimension of alignment as an important variable that affects the dependent variable - the intellectual dimension of IT- business alignment. Based on these assumptions, the authors explore the processes of IT and business management, believing that well-built processes between IT and business also "even out" the gap between these departments. The authors introduce some special mechanisms into the model, which, in their opinion, should have a strong correlation on the social dimension:

• Regular meetings between IT and business
• Rotation between departments

The point is to evaluate such mechanisms in the company under study, their arrangement to analyze the effectiveness.

Scientists, studying this issue [2, 3], rely on the framework proposed in [8]. This study of causes, factors of alignment has been extensively researched in the process of creating a starting point in the study of strategic business planning. Therefore, the proposed template is often used by researchers to introduce and develop the concepts of dimensions, dimensions of IT business alignment (see Table 2).

3 Development of a Theoretical Model Based on Nomological Networks

The concept of "nomological network" was first introduced in 1955 by the psychologists Cronbach and Paul Meehl [9]. They suggested that to prove the validity of the assumption, it is necessary to build a "nomological network". This is a representation of concepts, entities, as well as relationships between them, which are important in theoretical research. To build a network, several conditions are necessary [1, 9]:

1. At least two objects under study - constructs
2. Theoretical assumptions that are expressed in relationships between constructs
3. Measurement rules
4. Hypotheses for data collection

Relationships between elements must obey "rules", which may be causal or statistical. The development of the nomological network of a construct is the study and refinement of knowledge about the construct. The development of ideas about the construct is associated with the addition of new relationships, either between existing elements of the network or between these elements and new elements outside the network [1].

The idea of a nomological network expands the usual context of measuring the social dimension of IT-business alignment, which, because of measurements, are not presented as separate dimensions, but are included in a certain space of interrelated factors. The selection of a particular construct depends on the premises of a particular theory.

The study of the application of the tool of nomological networks for the study of information technology is considered in the work [17]. The authors provide a systematic analysis of how researchers use the capabilities of this tool, and make an attempt to classify these works.

The authors [11] of the work developed a process based on statistical data that automatically solves the nomological network, that is, evaluates the influence of factors on the dependent variable. Thus, we can conclude that to prove the hypotheses that are used in the nomological network, the statistical apparatus of analysis is often used, in a particular case, a machine learning tool.

To solve the problem of the social dimension of alignment, this tool has already been used [14] to express theoretical assumptions on the sources of this dimension. However, this work, as a data source, uses a survey of IT and business managers.

In a previous study [13] it was suggested that by looking for intersection in terms of IT business artifacts, the degree of IT business alignment can be measured. After conducting a primary analysis of artifacts for the correspondence of terms at a certain stage of the business process, a method for searching for the social dimension of IT-business alignment was formalized.

In this paper, the study was designed in a way to theoretically show the premises, using conceptual modeling methods along with nomological networks. The figure shows an exploratory model that represents the prerequisites and the dependent variable - a common language that affects the social dimension of alignment (Fig. 2).

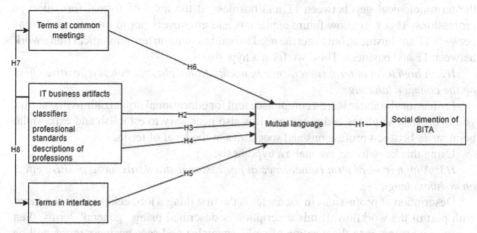

Fig. 2. Theoretical model with the usage of nomological network

Reasons for the emergence of the social dimension of alignment:

1. Compliance at the level of IT-business artifacts
2. Compliance at the interface level
3. Compliance at the level of meetings between IT and business

By highlighting the main terms in each of the prerequisites, it is possible to fix the boundaries of a certain type of activity, and with a high percentage of coincidence of these terms, it can be argued that the level of social alignment increases. Considering that a common language is an important factor in achieving a common understanding, and further to a common IT-business agreement, it must be assumed that there is an explicit way to achieve this understanding. These methods are the prerequisites presented in figure.

To correspond to the structure of the nomological network, it is necessary to define theoretical assumptions - hypotheses.

The common language between IT and business is the ability to build joint plans [2, 10, 15], not waste time searching for common meanings, and reduce the time to achieve common goals. Thus, we can hypothesize:

H1: Common language between IT and business has a positive effect on the social dimension of the IT-business alignment.

Classifiers are used everywhere. This is a special structured list of elements. From the point of view of the classifier of professions, it is necessary for the following tasks:

1. Structuring information about professions

2. Qualification control - the ability to formally define the boundaries between qualifications, areas of work
3. Statistical analysis of occupations

The purpose of using classifiers to search for IT-business inconsistencies is to reduce the terminological gap between IT and business at the level of formal formation of professions. This will allow future applicants and employers not to invent interactions between IT and business, but to get the need to build a common terminological framework between IT and business. Thus, we form a hypothesis:

H2: A high level of term coincidence in occupational classifiers has a positive effect on the common language.

Professional standards are a compliance tool for educational organizations that allows you to create disciplines and programs. It is also necessary to establish and expand the boundaries between professions and specialties at the level of terms.

Using this knowledge, we make a hypothesis:

H3: A high level of term coincidence in professional standards has a positive effect on common language.

Description of professions in vacancies is the first thing a job seeker sees when faced with part of the workflow. If this description is described using "general" terms, then a person who comes to the position of an IT specialist and sees business terms will be required to study these terms even before hiring. In this way, he will receive a part of this common language that promotes alignment.

H4: A high level of term coincidence in job descriptions has a positive effect on common language.

It has previously been suggested that the interfaces used by business and IT may be an expression of the social dimension of the IT-Business alignment [14]. For example, terms on specific action buttons that are developed by IT for business and shared, for example, in administrative panels, may be misunderstood by the business. Because of this, not only problems in misunderstanding are possible, but real problems for the client. So, for example, assigning a status to a user in which he cannot enter his personal account is called "merge into ballast". What should a representative of the client department think when he sees such a phrase? Is it necessary to use a word that both IT and business can understand? Such questions should be asked when analyzing interface elements.

H5: A high level of term coincidence on interface elements that are shared between IT and business has a positive effect on common language.

The study of the terminological apparatus at meetings of IT and business will allow the development of a special terminological language that will reduce the gap in the mismatch between IT and business. So, the hypothesis goes like this:

H6: Sharing, a high level of term coincidence during IT and business meetings has a positive effect on the common language.

The following assumptions are relationships between model assumptions:

H7: With high usage of common terms in IT business artifacts, sharing of terms in meetings increases.

H8: High use of common terms in IT business artifacts increases term overlap on interface elements.

The proposed hypotheses entail obvious management decisions that affect each factor.

The tool of nomological networks is applied to the task of searching and analyzing the social dimension of IT-business alignment to formalize the prerequisites. Thus, in the ideal case, when the social dimension of IT-business alignment is at a high level, all 8 hypotheses in the structure of the theoretical model are fulfilled. If at least one of the hypotheses is not fulfilled, then the management must make an appropriate management decision, which should lead to the implementation of the problematic hypothesis.

The structure of the nomological network is built in such a way that the main prerequisite for the social dimension of IT-business alignment is a common language. The high impact of common language on the social dimension of IT-Business alignment has been proven by statistical models in several papers [5, 12, 13]. Thus, the hypothesis H1 is fulfilled by default. However, the prerequisites for achieving a common language were not formalized. In this paper, it is assumed that formal correspondence, the coincidence of terms in artifacts, meetings, interfaces, is the factor that contributes to the formation of a common language.

Exploring the conceptual way of analyzing the social dimension of IT-Business alignment [14], it was assumed that the use of common terms in classifiers allows you to identify a pool of professions that contribute to IT-Business alignment. So, the process of issuing a loan in one of the largest banks in Russia was analyzed. Having decomposed the process into its constituent parts, it was found that in the professions of this process, which are described in classifiers, reference books, the terms have a high intersection. Thus, we believe that the hypotheses H2, H3, H4, H8 are fulfilled.

Analyzing the interface of the common interface - the admin panel, it was found that all the terms that are used on functional elements are not universal for IT and business. That is, when interacting with these elements, misunderstandings on the part of IT and business are possible. Hypothesis H5 is fulfilled. Hypotheses H6 and H7 are not fulfilled by default since IT development was not invited to business meetings.

Possible managerial influences are suggested that will reduce the gap between the IT business, with the subsequent implementation of hypotheses.

4   Result and Discussion

In this paper, the basis for a theoretical model was presented using the toolkit of nomological networks. Using networks, one can theoretically prove the validity of the model, and subsequently statistically prove hypotheses and relationships between entities. Thus, this work is an important extension of past research that will allow a more systematic approach to future research on the social dimension of IT-Business alignment.

They are also expanding the research methodology, which in most cases was based on a survey method of data collection. The use of conceptual research methods entails a deeper understanding of causal relationships and analysis of their impact on the social dimension of IT-Business alignment. Given the growing interest in the alignment problem, as well as the widespread use of big data tools, this work can be used as a theoretical basis for statistical research.

Table 2. Management actions

Management action	Result
Collaborative discussion of terms that are used in the interface	Increase common understanding between IT and business
Develop job descriptions using terms that are used by business and IT	The degree of social dimension of IT-Business alignment will increase from the early stages of the process
Use internal classifiers with revised description	Increasing terminological coincidence, which leads to its increase in other areas of the enterprise
Conduct educational activities that are aimed at increasing general erudition in IT and business	Increase understanding of plans and strategies by IT and business
Invitation of IT and business specialists to general meetings on plans and strategies	Collaborative development of IT and business terms, which will increase the alignment of IT and business

References

1. Artemenkov, S.L.: Network modeling of psychological constructs. Netw. Model. Psychol. Constr. **1**, 9–28 (2017)
2. Hütter, A., Arnitz, T., Riedl, R.: Effective CIO/CEO Communication Conference Paper; August 2020
3. Becker, W., Schmid, O.: The right digital strategy for your business: an empirical analysis of the design and implementation of digital strategies in SMEs and LSEs. Bus. Res. **13**(3), 985–1005 (2020). https://doi.org/10.1007/s40685-020-00124-y
4. Reich, B.H., Benbasat, I.: Measuring the linkage between business and information technology objectives. MIS Q. **20**(1), 55–81 (1996). https://doi.org/10.2307/249542
5. Reich, B.H., Benbasat, I.: Factors that influence the social dimension of alignment between business and information technology objectives. MIS Q. **24**(1), 81–113 (2000)
6. Carvalho, R., Sousa, P.: Business and information systems misalignment model (BIS-MAM): an holistic model leveraged on misalignment and medical sciences approaches. Proc. BUSITAL **8**, 105 (2008)
7. Chi, M., Huang, R., George, J.F.: Collaboration in demand-driven supply chain: based on a perspective of governance and IT-business strategic alignment. Int. J. Inf. Manage. **52**, 102062 (2020)
8. Pelletier, C., Croteau, A.-M., Raymond, L., Vieru, D.: Achieving social IT alignment through the orchestration of it assets: an interpretive case study. Inf. Syst. Manag. **38**(1), 42–61 (2021). https://doi.org/10.1080/10580530.2020.1733712
9. Cronbach, L.J., Meehl, P.E.: Construct validity in psychological tests. Psychol. Bull. **52**(4), 281–302 (1955). https://doi.org/10.1037/h0040957.hdl:11299/184279.PMID13245896
10. Henderson, J.C., Venkatraman, N.: Strategic alignment: leveraging information technology for transforming organizations. IBM Syst. J. **32**(1), 4–17 (1993)
11. Li, J., Larsen, K.R.: Establishing nomological networks for behavioral science: a natural language processing based approach. In: Proceedings of the 32nd International Conference on Information Systems, Shanghai, China (2011)

12. Luftman, J.: Assessing IT/business alignment. Inf. Syst. Manag. **20**(4), 9–15 (2003). https://doi.org/10.1201/1078/43647.20.4.20030901/77287.2
13. Luftman, J., Lyytinen, K., Zvi, T..: Enhancing the measurement of informationtechnology (IT) business alignment and its influence on company performance. J. Inf. Technol. **32**, 26–46 (2017)
14. Khlebnikov, R., Malyzhenkov, P.: A new approach to the social dimension of IT business alignment. In: Polyvyanyy, A., RinderleMa, S. (eds.) Advanced Information Systems Engineering Workshops. LNBIP, vol. 423, pp. 59–68. Springer, Cham (2021). https://doi.org/10.1007/978-3-030-79022-6_6
15. Preston, D.S., Karahanna, E.: Antecedents of IS strategic alignment: a nomological network. Inf. Syst. Res. **20**(2), 159–179 (2009)
16. Schlosser, F.: Mastering the social IT/business alignment challenge. In: 18th Americas Conference on Information Systems 2012, AMCIS 2012, pp. 1843–1849. United States: AIS Electronic Library (2012)
17. Belkhamza, Z., Hubona, G.S.: Nomological Networks in IS Research. Emergent Research Forum (ERF) (2018)

E-resources

18. https://www.techtarget.com/searchcio/feature/CIOs-can-avoid-tech-hype-with-business-IT-alignment
19. https://www.signavio.com/post/business-it-alignment-2021/
20. https://www.globaliim.com/global-it-trends-researc

Design and Development of a Reconfigurable Enterprise Financial Reporting Service

Boris Ulitin[✉] , Eduard Babkin , Tatiana Babkina , and Igor Ulitin

HSE University, Nizhny Novgorod, Russia
{bulitin,eababkin,tbabkina,iulitin}@hse.ru

Abstract. This study aims to design and develop a reconfigurable enterprise financial reporting service. The product solutions available do not allow creating custom reports tailored to the needs of each enterprise. The paper provides a detailed analysis of the types of the company's financial report and a comparison of existing services according to some criteria. The research contains information about the current products solutions, their benefits and drawbacks, which can be applied for achieving the goal. Furthermore, it comprises a definition of the solution architecture with the designation of the technology stack and the prototype functionality.

Keywords: BPMN · Finance · Financial report · Reconfigurable service

1 Introduction

Compliance with the requirements of sustainable development is an essential task of modern enterprises [1]. This task becomes even more urgent in the context of companies adhering to the principles of lean production [2]. The combination of these concepts results in a diversified and steady development of all branches of activity and influence of the enterprise, from economic sustainability to social responsibility.

This is all the more relevant in the context of the Industry 4.0 paradigm, the main aspect of which is the maximum automation of all enterprise processes, from production to reporting [1]. And the main element of automation in the case of complex enterprise processes is the introduction of systems with elements of business intelligence (BI) [4]. However, in this case, there is a need to develop convenient mechanisms for interacting with such BI-systems, since in the process of preparing reports on sustainable development, a comprehensive analysis of all available indicators of enterprise performance is required.

For the most part, various BI-systems can be used to calculate these indicators, including complex algorithms based on data from the company's financial and accounting statements. But only as long as there is no need to modify the existing set of indicators. Any modification of the report results in the need to change the entire set of indicators and algorithms for their calculation. Moreover, each such change needs additional verification and approval, since it affects indicators that are public. As a result, the reporting process becomes time-consuming and inefficient [2]. Furthermore, most current services

E. Babkin et al. (Eds.): MOBA 2022, LNBIP 457, pp. 84–99, 2022.
https://doi.org/10.1007/978-3-031-17728-6_8

cannot provide the end-user with the flexibility and simplicity facilitating the creation of management and other financial reports, which leads to the need to use tools that are not designed for that or to look for workarounds [5].

This completely contradicts the ideas of lean manufacturing, which are also characteristic of the concept of sustainable development [2]. Based on this, we come to the conclusion that methods are needed to simplify the process of modifying the system of indicators used in the preparation of the sustainability report.

There are some attempts to introduce elements of adaptation into reporting systems. For example, Smirnova et al. in [5] propose to use not only individual indicators, but also cumulative metrics that can be modified in the course of the company's operation.

However, this change is carried out at the system backend level and cannot be implemented by the end-user without the help of the developer.

Another alternative is to use complex financial reporting systems that include various services and modules. However, such systems are expensive and require the creation of a single information ecosystem at the enterprise [14]. As a consequence, such solutions are available only for large enterprises, but not for small and medium-sized ones [11]. This limitation is primarily due to the fact that small and medium-sized companies prefer to use a set of highly specialized solutions for various tasks, including for reporting.

However, such limited tools lead to a lack of flexibility. As a result, companies are forced to either choose a complex, expensive solution or develop their own tools.

On the other hand, the definition of performance indicators is nothing more than a mathematical operation and therefore only leads to the appearance of an associated user interface input field. From this point of view, to determine your own performance indicators, you can use the mechanisms of evolution of the graphical user interface, based on its object-oriented representation and the relationship of various input elements with data fields.

In this case, the modification of the set of indicators is reduced to the need to determine the mathematical operations by means of which the indicator is calculated and their subsequent saving. This approach resembles the mechanisms of invariants, when we, while maintaining a set of basic structures, change the set of operations in which these structures are involved [18].

However, in this case, the modification of indicators is carried out through the interface and avoids the need to redefine the system as a whole at the source code level. In this paper, we demonstrate the main provisions of this approach and demonstrate its application using the example of a simplified application for generating reporting forms.

This article describes our approach and presents results as follows. In Sect. 2 we observe the main types of financial statements of enterprises. Section 3 contains information about reporting process in general as a stage of the company's activity. Section 4 is devoted to the architecture solutions, which will be used in the reporting service. Sections 5 and 6 contain basic information on the architecture and use cases of the developed system, as well as the results of evaluating its quality and efficiency. We conclude the article with an analysis of the proposed approach and further research steps.

2 Literature Review

The research on intelligent decision support systems for banking dates back to over four decades. Latest industry reports suggest 25% of new U.S. bank customers switch service providers within the first 12 months, half churn before 90 days [2]. Hence, this poses the question; what has gone wrong? It could be a lack of a 360-degree view of the customer, operational silos in internal data, poor customer experience, or rising costs. The Boston consulting group, 2019 report says that the USA, Germany, etc. are behind European nations like Spain, Poland, Netherlands, or Australia in digital sales-readiness [4].

While E-banking became popular in developing markets, heterogeneity of firms necessitates more study of their efficacy due to decision paradox on adoption [3]. As shown recently, West-centric service value scales adoption applies only moderately precisely in developing markets. Using generalized assumptions also accelerates the digital divide that hampers financial services from sustainable goals [5]. From the service provider's view, changes like ATMs replaced human tellers for repetitive cash withdraws and deposits, reducing human interventions. Hence, it's paramount to identify the operations for efficient information management in banking.

When determining the criteria for assessing the risk of transactions, financial institutions select organizations according to the criteria of the availability of financial services with the exception of organizations that do not meet the specified requirements. This is especially evident in the conditions of "greening" the economy and social integration. These two phenomena, related to the environmental and social pillars of sustainable development, respectively, strongly influence the need to expand risk assessment through the financial institutions' criterion for ESG (environmental, social and corporate governance) risk.

As a result, there is a need to develop flexible tools that make it possible to simplify the calculation of various indicators of organizations' performance for subsequent risk assessment.

This becomes even more important in the context of the ever-increasing complexity of the business models of organizations. A more complex organization model leads to a longer risk analysis and results in the likelihood of misjudging all aspects of the business. Currently, business models for companies to achieve their sustainability goals are becoming sustainable business models [12]. Sustainable business models leverage firms to integrate their economic objectives with their sustainability ambitions in such a way that the benefits of all stakeholders are achieved simultaneously [13, 14]. Porter and Kramer [15] argued that sustainable business models are sources of competitive advantage, in which incorporating sustainable value propositions, value creation, and value capturing mechanisms bear economic benefits to the companies. The capability of a fast and successful shift into new business models is one of the most important determinants of sustainable competitive advantage and is a factor leveraging the sustainability performance of organizations [15].

Developing a sustainable business model could be supported by a "brown taxonomy", the development of which has been recommended by the Technical Expert Group (TEG) on Sustainable Finance [16]. A "Brown taxonomy" could help companies to explain how they are reducing the negative impacts of their business activities as they try to become more sustainable [17].

Furthermore, the increasing volume and complexity of international accounting standards (IASs) prompted International Standards of Accounting and Reporting (ISAR) to consider the special accounting and reporting needs of small and medium-sized enterprises (SMEs). IFRS for SMEs, as a common international framework and standard, is adopted by many jurisdictions. However, there is also a diversity of frameworks on accounting for SMEs, which poses challenges with regard to comparability and quality of such reports. Unfortunately, existing scorecards [3, 10] are examples of large-scale systems that lack flexibility. Any change in one of the components forces you to adjust other indicators and the system as a whole. As a consequence, the report preparation process is laborious and time consuming.

The consolidation requirement in IFRS for SMEs is problematic due to a lack of accounting expertise in SMEs and accounting for extended payment terms. Other reasons include: costs of implementation; information technology issues; people issues; identification of temporary differences for deferred tax; lack of training and up-to-date knowledge; and the change from national standards to international standards, and the IFRS for SMEs, still seems too complicated and costly for SMEs [17].

There are also some technical challenges, for example the need to align the main recognition and measurement requirements for SMEs. The solution in this case may be the ability to develop a reporting service with the ability to the real-time reconfiguration, which allows not to collect their various indicators, but also to determine them using a special constructor. In this paper, we propose a system with such a functionality. Before describing the main features of the system as a whole, it is necessary to consider the types of reporting and their features.

3   Analysis of Reporting Types

Regardless of which organizations we are talking about and in which country they operate, all companies provide two types of reports based on the results of their activities: accounting and tax reporting [9]. However, almost every organization or enterprise approves management reporting for itself.

Accounting (financial) statements contain information about the financial position of an economic entity at the reporting date, the financial result of its activities and cash flows for the reporting period, systematized in accordance with the requirements established by different laws and standards. Accounting (financial) statements consist of the balance sheet, the profit and loss statement, the appendices to them provided for by the regulations, the audit report or the conclusion of the audit union of agricultural cooperatives and the explanatory note.

Basic requirements for the preparation and submission of the accounting financial report are the following:

- Taxpayers are required to submit annual accounting (financial) statements to the tax authorities at their place of residence;
- Reports are submitted to the tax authority no later than three months after the end of the reporting year;
- Reports must include performance indicators of all branches, representative offices and other divisions;

- The content and forms of organization of the balance sheet, profit and loss statement, other reports and appendices should be applied consistently from one reporting period to another;
- For each numerical indicator of the financial statements, except for the report prepared for the first reporting period, the data must be provided for at least two years – the reporting and the preceding reporting period;
- Accounting statements are compiled, stored and presented to users in the prescribed form on paper. In the presence of technical capabilities and with the consent of users of accounting statements, the organization can submit accounting statements in electronic form.

In addition to the previous points, each part of the financial statements must contain the following data:

- The name of the part;
- Indication of the reporting date or the reporting period for which the financial statements are prepared;
- The name of the organization with the indication of its organizational and legal form;
- The format of presentation of numerical indicators of accounting statements.

Tax reporting is a set of documents that are required to be submitted to the tax authorities after reporting periods or upon the occurrence of specific events [10].

Management reporting (including a sustainability report) is a set of internal reports of the enterprise, which are formed voluntarily. The main purpose of this type of reporting is to obtain reliable information about the state of affairs of the enterprise on a specific date, for example, to be provide to the management or owners of the enterprise It is management reporting that is most attractive and important for each enterprise. This type of reporting is most important for each company because it can and should be compiled and customized specifically for the needs of the company. An example would be a profit and loss statement for each business process within a company. This type of report ensures visualization of each stage of the business process and identifies bottlenecks or places where the greatest losses occur. Therefore, the services that help to compile this type of reporting are popular and highly demanded in the market.

Likewise, the sustainability report includes many heterogeneous performance indicators (currently over 200), grouped in accordance with 3 main directions of the enterprise development strategy: economic sustainability, environmental sustainability, social sustainability [4, 5]. Furthermore, each section is interconnected with others and is based on their results. For example, indicators of economic sustainability are based on economic, financial and tax performance indicators presented in other company reports. As a result, manual preparation of a sustainability report leads to duplication of work on preparation of other reports.

That is the reason why taking into account the heterogeneity of the used indicators and reports in general, it is necessary to propose a mechanism that allows you to dynamically enter new indicators of the enterprise reporting on the basis of integrated reports.

In order to develop such a universal mechanism, it is necessary to consider the reporting process as a whole, which will be discussed in the following section.

4   Analysis of the Reporting Process

After analyzing the components of the basic reports of the enterprise, it is important to understand how the process of their formation takes place in typical companies that can be attributed to small businesses.

For example, consider the process of preparing management reports in a small cleaning company. The process of preparing management reports (AS IS) took place with the participation of two people: an accountant and a financial director (Fig. 1). The accountant took 2 days to complete the tasks, while the CFO took about 2 h to complete the tasks.

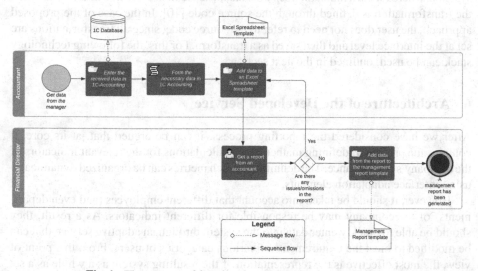

Fig. 1. The process of forming the management report (AS IS)

It can be seen from the presented process that in the case of the basic reporting process, many processes, despite the presence of automation elements, require laborious work of programmers. In particular, the stage of choosing a reporting document implies the preliminary development of a separate sheet in the reporting system.

However, since reporting consists of many separate indicators, we can generalize this process by preparing separate indicators instead of reporting sheets and combining them into a single report at the import stage. This will allow not only to optimize the process, eliminating the need to prepare separate reporting sheets, but also to make it more flexible by adding the ability to calculate your own reporting indicators based on the already created ones.

5   The Approach Proposed

As mentioned above, in our case of defining various metrics, we adhere to the following mathematical formalization.

Let there be a set of indicators of enterprise activity $Mark = \{mark_i\}, i = 1..N, N \in \mathbb{N}$. Then the metric of enterprise activity is defined as any function over the Mark set: $M = F(Mark)$.

In this case, the definition of the activity metric is reduced to the definition of the necessary transformation in the form of a mathematical formula.

On the other hand, any interface also consists of a set of input and output fields corresponding to one or another activity indicator. As a result, to define own metrics, the user only needs to provide a constructor that contains a list of available indicators and mathematical operations on them.

This differs from the generally accepted approaches found in existing reporting systems, where for each indicator a separate database element is created initially, and then the transformation is defined through the source code [10]. In the case of the proposed approach, the user does not need to refer to the source code, since all transformations are set at the interface level and then saved as a transform. For this, the following technology stack can be used, outlined in the next section.

6   Architecture of the Developed Service

After we have considered the reporting process, it can be argued that, at its core, it contains the process of defining mathematical calculations for the relevant indicators of the company's performance. The definition of such metrics can be organized dynamically using interface adaptation elements.

However, it should be taken into account that different employees (and even departments) of the company may be responsible for different indicators. As a result, they should be able to quickly enter data into the system through an adaptive service that can be modified to meet the requirements of various categories of users. From this point of view, the most effective is the representation of the resulting system as a whole as a set of services integrated with each other.

Software-as-a-Service (SaaS) is a software licensing model in which access to software is provided on a subscription basis, with the software located on external servers rather than internal ones. The software as a service is usually accessed via a web browser, with users logging in using a username and password. Instead of each user having to install the software on their own computer, the user can access the program via the Internet.

SaaS offers many **advantages** over traditional software licensing models. Since the software does not live on the servers of the licensing company, the demand for investment in new hardware is reduced. It's easy to implement, easy to update and debug, and can be less expensive (or at least have lower upfront costs) because users pay for SaaS as they come in, rather than buying multiple software licenses for multiple computers.

SaaS has many uses, including:

- Email services;
- Audit activities;
- Automation of registration of goods and services;
- Document management, including file sharing and document collaboration;

- Shared corporate calendars that you can use to plan events;
- Customer relationship Management (CRM) systems, which are essentially a database of information about customers and potential customers. SaaS-based CRM can be used to store company contact information, business activity, purchased products, and lead tracking.

The types of software ported to the SaaS model are often focused on enterprise-level services, such as human resources management. These types of tasks are often collaborative, requiring employees from different departments to share, edit, and publish materials without necessarily being in the same office.

Disadvantages of SaaS

The **disadvantages** of implementing **SaaS** are related to data security and the speed of its delivery. Since the data is stored on external servers, companies need to be sure that it is secure and cannot be accessed by unauthorized persons. A slow Internet connection can reduce performance, especially if the cloud servers are accessed from a long distance. Internal networks tend to be faster than internet connections.

Like most software systems, a service-oriented system is based on a triplet **Model-View-Controller** (**MVC**). **MVC** is an architectural pattern that divides an application into three main logical components: model, view, and controller. Each of these components is designed to handle specific aspects of application development. MVC is one of the most commonly used industry standard web development frameworks for creating scalable and extensible projects.

This separation of logic between the three components makes the system as a whole more efficient and allows the various components to be modified independently of each other, which is essential for the planned reconfigurable service.

From a technical point of view and taking into account the need to provide ubiquitous access to the developed service, the web architecture of the developed solution seems to be optimal. Based on this, the use of technologies such as Vue.js [5], Node.js [6], ExpressJS [7] and Docker [8].

Vue.js is JavaScript library for creating web interfaces using the MVVM architecture template (Model-View-View-Model) [5]. Since Vue.js only works at the "view level" and is not used for middleware and hardware-software applications, it can be easily integrated with other projects and libraries. Vue.js contains broad view-level functionality and can be used to build powerful single-page web applications.

However, in our work, we will use Vue.js, because it has a number of the following advantages over AngularJS and React, in particular:

- Vue.js is easier to learn and is in no way inferior in performance to the React and Angular frameworks.
- Incredibly light weight Vue.js, since the data that is executed on the user side can easily be presented on the server side at the same time.
- Easy and convenient testing of the built solution using Jest. While Anuglar uses the Jasmine test software framework.

Node.js is an open-source cross-platform JavaScript runtime that executes JavaScript code outside of the browser [6]. JavaScript is used primarily for client-side scripting, in which scripts written in JavaScript are embedded in the HTML of a web page and executed on the client side by the JavaScript engine in the user's web browser. Node.js allows developers to use JavaScript to write command-line tools and for server-side scripting - running server-side scripts to create dynamic web page content before sending it to the user's web browser. Hence, Node.js is a "JavaScript everywhere" paradigm that combines web application development around a single programming language, rather than different languages for server-side and client-side scripting.

ExpressJS, or simply Express, is a de facto standard web application framework for Node.js, implemented as free and open-source software under the MIT license. It is designed to create web applications and APIs. The author of the software framework, TJ Holowaychuk, describes it as based on the Sinatra framework written in Ruby, implying that it is minimalistic and includes a large number of plugins [7].

Docker is software for automating the deployment and management of applications in containerization-enabled environments [8]. This tool allows users to store the application with all its environment and dependencies in a container that can be migrated to any Linux system with cgroups support in the kernel, and also provides a container management environment. Initially, I used the capabilities of LXC, and since 2015, I have used my own library that abstracts the virtualization capabilities of the Linux kernel—lib container. With the advent of the Open Container Initiative, the transition from a monolithic to a modular architecture began. In the course work, Docker is used as an emulator of the environment and servers in which the application will be stored and function.

Also, the decision to stop at Docker was made, due to the fact that this software has the ability to export the environment settings and use them on the operating environment.

Finally, given the need to store various data and metrics to eliminate the need to recalculate them, a database should be used. Industrial enterprises use large storage systems, however, for our prototype and for ease of demonstration of performance, we will use **PostgreSQL**, which is a free object-relational database management system (DBMS).

PostgreSQL differs from other DBMSs in its support for the popular object-oriented and/or relational approach to databases. For example, it guarantees full support for reliable transactions, i.e. Atomicity, Consistency, Isolation, Durability (ACID). Thanks to powerful technologies, PostgreSQL is very productive. Parallelism is achieved not by blocking read operations, but by implementing multivariate concurrency control (MVCC), which also ensures ACID compliance. PostgreSQL is very easy to extend with its own procedures, which are called stored procedures. These functions simplify the use of constantly repeated operations.

Finally, given the specifics of the application being developed, we cannot fail to mention security and data protection issues. Thanks to the use of modern frameworks, it is possible to implement quite heavy, complex, but at the same time, effective and modern security algorithms. On the server and database side, the AES-256-CBC encryption algorithm is used. This algorithm quickly and securely encrypts only string, numeric, and array data. It is important to note that in comparison with other encryption algorithms of the AES family, which are still used in various systems and services, this one requires the longest time to decrypt, namely 3.31 * 10^56 years to crack and 1.1 * 10^77 different combinations.

The use of these technologies will allow us to develop an effective application that meets goals from the beginning of the article: Development of a reconfigurable enterprise financial reporting service prototype.

Furthermore, the responsiveness of the reporting service user interface would be provided by the Vue.js framework features such as a set of ready-made UI components that can be easily used during development and features of CSS styles that can be used in this framework.

7   Practical Cases

In this chapter, the main algorithms and features of the developed financial reporting service will be considered, as well as the verification of the obtained solution on the example of a specific case.

7.1   Import Financial Operations from Banks

In order to export financial transactions from various banks, a special script is used that 'simulates' the behavior of the bank's mobile client and, due to this, allows you to quickly, easily and officially access the user's financial transactions. The simulation is carried out by using special headers (supposedly a mobile device, etc.).

First, the application requests the user's login data to the client bank. Then, in an encrypted HTTPS form, it passes it to the server. If the data is correct, it logs in and imports transactions from the client bank for the date period specified by the user (Fig. 2). Furthermore, the user can specify specific counterparties whose operations need to be imported using filters (Fig. 3). After exporting the data, the service server processes and converts the data into the required form, encrypts it, and adds it to the database.

Choose bank:

Fig. 2. Page for importing financial operations

7.2   Preparation of the Management Report

The management reports compilation in the service requires the end-user to set the necessary indicators that should appear in the generated report and to set the rules by which the data should be considered indicators and where the data for calculating indicators should be taken from.

In order to implement the above, it is necessary to go to the 'Create Indicator' page and start filling in the data (Fig. 4). The user needs to come up with a name for the indicators and create a formula for calculating the indicator. The formula is created by transferring the available elements to a special field for the formula.

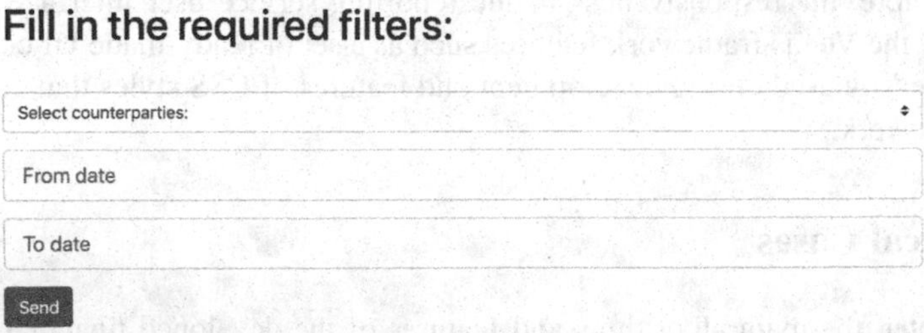

Fill in the required filters:

Select counterparties: ⬍

From date

To date

Send

Fig. 3. Page for selecting filters to be used for importing transactions from the bank

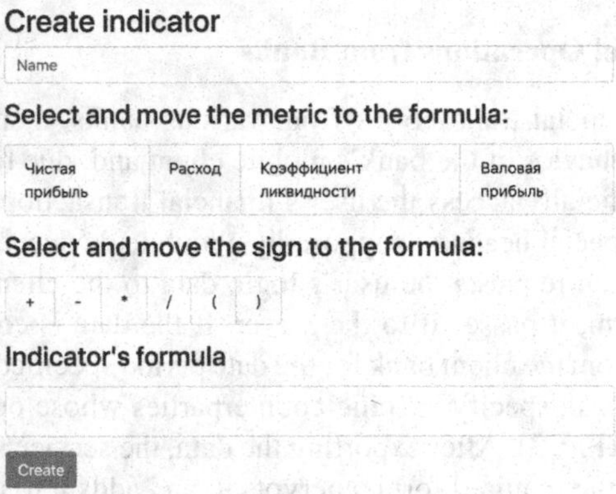

Create indicator

Name

Select and move the metric to the formula:

| Чистая прибыль | Расход | Коэффициент ликвидности | Валовая прибыль |

Select and move the sign to the formula:

+   -   *   /   (   )

Indicator's formula

Create

Fig. 4. 'Create indicator' page

After creating the management report template, the end-user only needs to click on the Export button to get the finished report, which can either be viewed online or downloaded as an XLSX file.

7.3 Specify the Reporting Indicators Directly in the BPMN Chart

In order to specify the indicators in the BPMN chart and track their dynamics, the end-user must first generate a management report inside the system and upload the file with the BPMN chart in a special format so that the service can perform the correct parsing of the file.

To upload a file with a BPMN chart, click on the 'Import chart' button and select the 'Browse' button on the page that opens and click 'Import' to download the BPNM file and then parse the downloaded file (Fig. 5, Fig. 6).

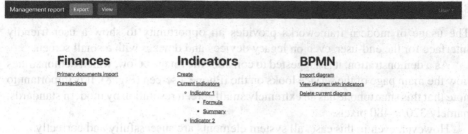

Fig. 5. Main page of the system

Import BPMN-diagram:

Fig. 6. The 'Import BPMN-diagram' page

After the BPMN diagram is uploaded, the user will need to connect the metrics and elements of the BPMN - diagram. As soon as the connection bundle is ready, the user will only need to open the page 'View a BPMN chart' to see the connection between metrics and chart elements (Fig. 7).

Viewing BPMN-diagram

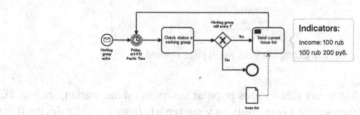

Fig. 7. The 'view a BPMN chart' page

Next, the user needs to select the desired task and select the desired indicator for it from the management report.

8 Evaluation and Validation of the System Developed

After considering the main scenarios of the developed system's behavior, it is necessary to analyze its advantages and limitations.

8.1 Flexibility of the Developed System

The usage of modern frameworks provides an opportunity to show a user-friendly interface for the end-user, even on legacy devices and devices with a small screen.

As a demonstration, it is suggested to consider the image below, which demonstrates how the main page of the service looks on the iPhone 4 screen (Fig. 8). It is important to note that this smartphone has an extremely small screen resolution by modern standards, namely 320 × 480 pixels.

However, even in this case, all system elements are successfully and correctly.

displayed on the screen and are available to the end-user without any errors, such as truncated text or inability to navigate the page. Such the ability to work with the system even though such a small screen speaks for the high flexibility and adaptability of the created system.

Fig. 8. The example of the main page opened on iPhone

It is also noticeable to say that various popular solutions on the market, such as 1C Accounting, do not provide the opportunity to view reports from a mobile device from any place in the world. Furthermore, almost none of the services on the market allows interacting simultaneously with BPMN diagrams and management reporting indicators.

8.2 The Effectiveness of the System

To assess the effectiveness of the developed system, we propose to consider the process of preparing management reports before the development of the system (AS IS) and the process of preparing management reports using the developed system (TO BE) on the example of one cleaning company.

As described above (Fig. 1), the management reporting process (AS IS) took 50 h of the time of two key employees of the company.

The process of drawing up management reports using the developed system (TO BE) takes place with the participation of the same two people (the accountant and the financial director), but contains much fewer tasks and, accordingly, takes much less time (Fig. 9). The accountant now takes 1 day to complete tasks, while the CFO now takes about 10 min to complete tasks.

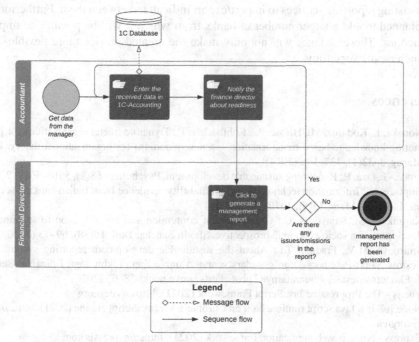

Fig. 9. The process of forming the management report (TO BE)

9 Conclusion

The preparation of various reports, ranging from financial to social, is an integral part of the concept of sustainable development [5]. Coupled with the ideas and principles of lean manufacturing, this concept requires a high degree of flexibility from the enterprise, including in the area of reporting.

In this paper we examined the process of preparing various types of financial statements at an enterprise and the possibilities for its customization and optimization through a reconfigurable service.

The need to develop this service is primarily due to the fact that in the presence of a large number of changing, heterogeneous performance indicators of an enterprise, it is very difficult to control the process of their calculation [2]. In the context of a sustainable development framework that includes more than 200 performance indicators, the ability to change the set of indicators is critical [4].

Unlike existing solutions [5], which only offer the ability to group already created indicators into cumulative metrics, the proposed service allows you to redefine a set of indicators and create new ones in real-time. This allows users to reduce the time for preparing reports and affects the agility of the entire enterprise in general.

In addition to flexibility in terms of indicators, the system supports the ability to integrate with business process analysis systems and import performance indicators into an enterprise process diagram.

In the future, it is planned to expand the service created with the ability to integrate with existing reporting services to import/export indicators between them. Furthermore, it is planned to add a larger number of banks from which it will be possible to import transactions. These changes will not only make the created service more flexible, but also increase its versatility.

References

1. Nonaka, I., Kodama, M., Hirose, A., Kohlbacher, F.: Dynamic fractal organizations for promoting knowledge-based transformation – a new paradigm for organizational theory. Eur. Manag. J. **32**(1), 137–146 (2014)
2. Japee, G., Oza, P.: Redefining sustainable development. Psychology **58**(2), 5610–5619 (2021)
3. Gupta, et al.: Information technology and profitability: evidence from Indian banking sector. Int. J. Emerg. Mark. **13**(5), 1070–1087 (2018)
4. Karthikvel, S., Samydoss, C.: Organizational contention and confrontation to sustainable development: a socio-economic prospective. Shodh Sanchar Bull. **10**(38), 69–73 (2020)
5. Smirnova, M.V., Fradina, T.I.: About the sustainable development reporting system. In: Vestnik Sankt-Peterburgskogo gosudarstvennogo universiteta tekhnologii i dizajna. Seriya 3: Ekonomicheskie, gumanitarnye i obshchestvennye nauki 58–63 (2020)
6. Vue.js - The Progressive JavaScript Framework (2021). https://vuejs.org
7. Node.js® is a JavaScript runtime built on Chrome's V8 JavaScript engine (2021). https://nodejs.org/en
8. Express - Node.js web application framework (2021). https://expressjs.com
9. Empowering App Development for Developers | Docke (2021). https://www.docker.com
10. Zavolochkina, L.: Principy formirovaniya finansovoj (buhgalterskoj) otchetnosti po mezhdunarodnym standartam buhgalterskoj otchetnosti i rossijskim standartam buhgalterskogo ucheta [Principles of formation of financial (accounting) statements according to international accounting standards and Russian accounting standards]. Biznes. Obrazovanie. Pravo **1**(11), 192–197 (2010)
11. Matveeva, T.: Bezbumazhnaya tekhnologiya sdachi nalogovoj i buhgalterskoj otchetnosti [Paperless technology for submitting tax and accounting reports], **2**, 16–19 (2003)
12. Nosratabadi, S., Mosavi, A., Shamshirband, S., Zavadskas, E.K., Rakotonirainy, A., Chau K.W.: Sustainable business models: a review. Sustainability **11**, 1663 (2019)
13. Abdelkafi, N., Täuscher, K.: Business models for sustainability from a system dynamics perspective. Organ. Environ. **29**, 74–96 (2016)
14. Morioka, S.N., Bolis, I., Evans, S., Carvalho, M.M.: Transforming sustainability challenges into competitive advantage: multiple case studies kaleidoscope converging into sustainable business models. J. Cleaner Prod. **167**, 723–738 (2017)
15. Porter, M.E., Kramer, M.R.: The big idea: creating shared value. Harv. Bus. Rev. **89**, 62–77 (2011)
16. Hurley, M.: EU's TEG: Develop 'brown' taxonomy to support energy transition. Environmental Finance (2020). https://www.environmentalfinance.com/content/news/eus-teg-develop-brown-taxonomy-to-support-energy-transition.html. Accessed 2 May 2021

17. Lester, A.: Role of ESG in credit risk analysis is growing, despite data drag. Environmental Finance (2020a). https://www.environmentalfinance.com/content/news/role-of-esg-in-credit-risk-analysis-is-growing-despite-data-drag.html. Accessed 3 May 2021
18. Ulitin, B., Babkin, E., Babkina, T., Vizgunov, A.: Automated formal verification of model transformations using the invariants mechanism. In: Pańkowska, M., Sandkuhl, K. (eds.) BIR 2019. LNBIP, vol. 365, pp. 59–73. Springer, Cham (2019). https://doi.org/10.1007/978-3-030-31143-8_5

Using Self-paced Multimedia Courses to Create Individual Student Trajectories

A. S. Adzhemov[⊠], I. V. Manonina, and V. V. Shestakov

Moscow Technical University of Communications and Informatics, 111024 Moscow, Russia
asa@mtuci.ru

Abstract. The connection between the learning process should have a close inter-action with changes in the student's personality, manifested in a change in the structure of educational motivation and the hierarchy of motives; in the formation of such value orientations as interesting work, knowledge, productive life, education, responsibility, efficiency in business; in the formation of readiness for self-development and adequate self-esteem. The formation of an adequate self-esteem is very important, since a student's critical attitude towards himself will allow him to competently correlate his own strengths and capabilities with tasks of various difficulties and with the requirements of the people around him. In addition, this will allow in the future to successfully master new digital competencies, to have a flexible orientation of the individual in the digital professional world. The goals set cannot be carried out in the course of mass training for the formation of a creative style of professional activity.

To this end, the authors propose to develop an information and technical program model that reflects the basis for creating a system for constructing individual educational trajectories of students, using SMART technologies based on artificial intelligence. In addition, such a model can be used to create inclusive training and testing complexes for persons with disabilities based on SMART-technologies. To do this, it is necessary to take into account the existing experience, established traditions, the ability to perceive new things, the readiness to use modern various infocommunication solutions in the organization of education, not only of the students, but also of their teachers, as well as the readiness of the corresponding educational and methodological materials. Thus, it is required to form not only educational and methodological materials, but also an adequate control and measuring environment that allows one to obtain objective assessments that characterize the process of studying the discipline and the quality of mastering the material.

When implementing the specified information and technical software model, it is necessary to ensure the timing of the study time of the material and answers. And also the ability to fix and record the number of correct, erroneous and missed answers during testing, followed by the formation of a report, which reflects the time spent on the tests, the total number of questions asked, the number of incorrect answers, as well as the numbers (or text with the task) of those questions where mistakes were made and so on. And the development of adaptive methods for data analysis will draw the attention of students to the existing gaps in their knowledge and pay more attention to re-studying the exact section where mistakes were made.

© The Author(s), under exclusive license to Springer Nature Switzerland AG 2022
E. Babkin et al. (Eds.): MOBA 2022, LNBIP 457, pp. 100–109, 2022.
https://doi.org/10.1007/978-3-031-17728-6_9

Development of recommendations for the use of the accumulated information, which, depending on the goals and methodological tasks to be solved, can be displayed on the screen, printed out, or saved as a file, should be available for further analysis. This will make it possible to form an individual portrait of the learner, which will be the initial data for the adequate work of "artificial intelligence", performing a controlling, consulting and teaching role.

Keywords: Individual student portrait · Individual educational trajectory of a student · Interaction · SMART technologies · Testing

1 Introduction

The research is aimed at solving the fundamental interdisciplinary problem of individual educational trajectories of students, taking into account their cognitive and personal capabilities. The fundamental nature of this task is justified by the fact that in the presence of various information and technical solutions, there is currently no general model of what parameters of students and the educational process an individual educational trajectory should take into account, how these parameters can be formalized to work with information technology systems, as possible the most effective use of information and technical means related to the category of SMART technologies based on artificial intelligence, for the formation of an individual educational trajectory of a student, as a kind of integral assessment of his work in the study of the discipline. And the accumulation of many such trajectories will allow the introduction of a comparison mechanism, as a result of which each student can be recommended to correct the learning trajectory if it is found to "fall out" from the nominally successful range. The development of such a model requires the involvement of specialists from various disciplinary fields, since it is necessary to take into account the cognitive-psychological, organizational-pedagogical and information-technical parameters of the developed model. The model is being developed in accordance with the modern educational trend, which is called "Smart-Education" [1–3].

2 General Information

The "Law on Education" indicates that the content of education is one of the factors of economic and social progress of society and should be focused on promoting: mutual understanding and cooperation between people, as well as taking into account the diversity of worldview approaches; to promote the realization of the right of students to a free choice of opinions and beliefs; to ensure the development of the abilities of each person, the formation and development of his personality in accordance with the spiritual, moral and sociocultural values adopted in the family and society. The content of vocational education must ensure the acquisition of qualifications [4].

In this regard, the problem of individualization is being actualized in the system of Russian higher education. An individual educational trajectory of a student (IETS) is a personal way of realizing the personal potential of each student in education, determined by the student together with the teacher, organized taking into account the motivation, abilities, mental, psychological and physiological characteristics of the student, as well as the socio-economic and temporal capabilities of the subject of educational process. Thus, IETS look like a personal way of realizing the student's potential in the educational process aimed at realizing individual aspirations, developing life strategies, forming the foundations of the individual, creative and professional development of the student's personality. The purpose of the IETS development is precisely to provide high-quality "piece" training of an individual specialist who is competent in the field of his professional activity and is in demand on the labor market. IETS has a spatio-temporal characteristic. This is a trajectory of an individual educational movement, a "trace" of a student's line of movement, formed by fixing the content of his tests and experience, educational achievements and characteristics of an individual educational space, which makes it possible to predict pedagogical and implement a tutor project.

The process of identifying, implementing and developing the cognitive, creative, and communicative abilities of trainees occurs during the educational movement of trainees along individual trajectories. A student will be able to advance along an individual trajectory if he is presented with the following opportunities: to choose the optimal forms and pace of learning; apply those teaching methods that are most consistent with his individual characteristics; to be reflexively aware of the results obtained, to assess and correct their activities.

In the process of training in an educational institution, an individual trajectory for achieving this goal is built by the student together with the teacher both with the help of existing and proposed elements for general training, and with the help of an additional set of methodological elements. Thus, the choice of the educational trajectory during the period of study at the university is the joint actions of the teacher and the student, aimed at developing the student's skills for independent educational activities, setting adequate educational goals and corresponding tasks, choosing methods, forms, means and content of training, reflection, self-assessment of personal achievements, initiative and responsibility for making decisions and solving tasks. Having learned to build individual educational trajectories during the period of study at the university, these skills and abilities will allow them, as necessary, to independently master the latest knowledge, to develop new skills of professional activity after graduating from an educational institution throughout their lives.

For the formation of IETS, the teacher plays a rather important role – he, together with the student, explains the rules and conditions of training, builds a learning trajectory, constantly monitors the student's educational activity, participates in assessing the results of this activity. As the learner gains experience in building an individual learning path, the degree of teacher participation in the student's learning decreases (but does not disappear). As a result of the repeated implementation of this methodology, each student must fully develop the ability to build his IETS in accordance with the needs and assigned tasks, it enables a specific student to choose the appropriate level of complexity of the material being studied. This will allow students with a low and medium level of proficiency in the discipline to study the material at an appropriate and accessible level, as well as students with a high level of intelligence and intentions to achieve a higher level of proficiency in the subject at the university, to fully realize their potential [5–7]. The implementation of the formation of such trajectories should be based on the professional preliminary work of the teacher, based on the study of advanced scientific, technical and technological achievements, which makes it possible to build a "tree" of education, where the central object on which everything else is formed is the textbook or its replacement content. But since the textbook or its replacement content contains a significant and detailed amount of information, it is advisable on their basis, using the capabilities of infocommunication systems, to prepare a more concentrated teaching material in the form of an electronic presentation, which includes additional software subsystems that provide "intellectual" support for the student.

It is important that this methodical implementation meets the initially set goals, that is, it provides a better understanding and assimilation of the discipline, and is not unnecessarily difficult to implement and, therefore, senselessly expensive [1, 8].

3 Creation of a Model Intellectual Trajectory of a Student and Program Implementation of a Lecture-Presentation

Along with electronic textbooks that most fully illuminate all the material under study, an electronic educational and methodological resource should be formed, for example, an electronic lecture-presentation with a built-in testing subsystem and with the possibility of intelligent processing of the results obtained, arising from measurements of various parameters that quantitatively characterize the learning process of students.

Having chosen a platform on which an intellectual electronic lecture-presentation will be implemented [9, 10], the next step is to fill it with educational and methodological material so that there is a possibility of its step-by-step study with fixing the quality of assimilation of the material in the form of certain quantitative indicators. Moreover, it is advisable to supplement a number of questions with increased complexity with multimedia moving objects, which will make it possible to more clearly explain and demonstrate all kinds of processes, which cannot always be reflected using static images. In addition, for a better perception of the studied material from the side of students, certain material can be voiced, which will significantly expand the information presented, give appropriate explanations or examples.

In order to be able to carry out a certain analysis of the student's behavior during the study of the discipline, it is necessary to enter a certain set of parameters by which the assessment is carried out (for example, the temporal characteristics of how long the student is "staying" on a particular educational block, how dynamically he responds to test questions, and so on) and a training trajectory is formed (see Fig. 1). It should be noted that it is important to know some initial data, allowing you to establish, as it were, the "origin of coordinates", relative to which subsequent actions and comparisons will be carried out. Of course, these inputs depend on the discipline being studied and must be determined by the course designer. However, it is possible to formulate a general set of such parameters that can be used in the formation of the scenario at the beginning, and then the course itself.

When working with a lecture-presentation, the student is identified, after which they are marked and entered in a separate table, generated automatically when the lecture-presentation is first accessed, the following data - the student's full name, group number

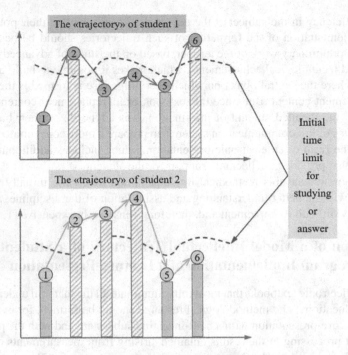

Fig. 1. Different "trajectories" of learning.

(see Fig. 2). In addition, the following is entered in the table: the date d_i^{ent} and T_i^{ent} time of the opening of the lecture-presentation (entry into the course), where i is the number of entry into the course. This table is created at the first access to the lecture-presentation, after which all other attempts are recorded in the specified table.

Further, it is necessary to determine some information blocks into which the teaching material of the course can be divided in order to properly control the study and assimilation of this content. In Fig. 1, these blocks numbered 1 through 6 are shown as rectangles. The dotted line is the initially set time that the student should spend studying this block. It is clear that reading and studying each of these blocks will take a certain amount of time, and this time will, as a rule, be different. The time is initially set by the course developer, based on his pedagogical experience and the complexity of the proposed material in the block. Later, after the accumulation of practical data, these times are specified, that is, there is a more adequate adjustment of the requirements, displayed by the dotted line, to the real practically obtained data on the trajectories of students.

Figure 1 shows the educational trajectories of some fictional students "Ivanov" and "Petrov". The initial conditions for these students are the same as indicated by the dotted line. However, in the course of studying the course, students show different time results of "staying" on certain blocks. Moreover, in Fig. 1, a circle around the number indicates the moments of transition from one block to another. Solid filled rectangles show blocks when students spent less time studying this block than originally envisaged, and diagonal filled rectangles show blocks when students spent more time studying this block, compared to the dotted line. Thus, the time spent on each element of the course is recorded, taking into account the number of entry into the course and the number of calls to this element (in this case, testing is excluded from this analysis and is considered separately). Let's denote this time by $t_i(n)$, where i is the number of entry into the course, and the value n is the number of the slide. Based on the teacher's experience, certain values of time are set, which, according to the developer, should be spent to study this element, that is, $t(n)$ is set as the norm for each of n slides, independent of i. The set of values $t_i(n)$ and $t(n)$ subsequently serve as a guideline when analyzing the dynamics of the course study from the side of the system and developing the corresponding " Recommendations and useful tips".

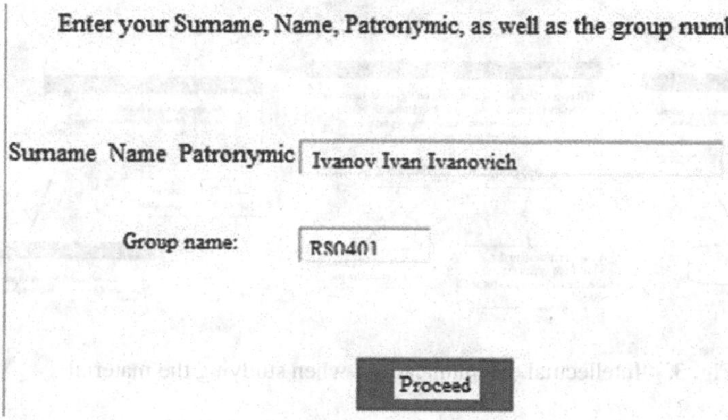

Enter your Surname, Name, Patronymic, as well as the group number.

Surname Name Patronymic | Ivanov Ivan Ivanovich

Group name: RS0401

Proceed

Fig. 2. Student identification

The lecture-presentation should provide for "intellectual communication" with the student. That is, when a student studies the proposed material, after the allotted control time, an intellectual "conversation" begins with the student. In the process of "communication" the student is asked various leading questions, the result of which is the identification of the reason why he is on this slide for a very long time: distracted by something, there is no interest in the material being studied, does not understand the material shown. Further, depending on the identified reason, the student is invited to either pay more attention to the study, or return to the initial slide, from which the study of this section began, in order to master the material again, or completely complete the study. The purpose of such "communication" is to attract the student's attention for a more attentive study and assimilation of the proposed content. Figure 3 shows an example of such "communication" with possible reactions to the identified reason for the long stay on the slide. At the same time, if the number of answers "There is no interest in studying" exceeds the permissible level, then the presentation with the studied material will be closed. The specified example has a two-level trajectory. But in order to obtain more complete information about the process of mastering the material by a student, such "communication" should be with more multilevel trajectories.

The testing subsystem built into the lecture-presentation should be built in a similar way, when students have to answer a number of questions, each of which is considered as a separate block and one or another time is spent on it. In addition, the testing subsystem records the number of attempts, the time and date of the start of testing, the duration of testing, the total number of questions, the number of questions missed, the number of correct answers, the number of errors made, the time norm for each question, and for each question its omission is marked/solution is correct/solution is incorrect. The data is recorded for all i-entries into the testing system.

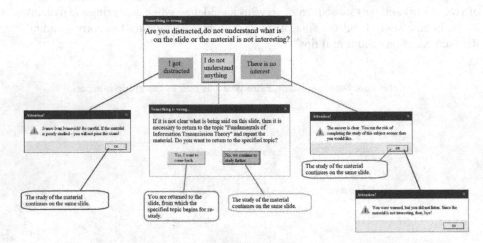

Fig. 3. "Intellectual communication" when studying the material

The testing subsystem should contain a different nature of the test task. In particular, the proposed tests can be divided into the following categories:

- A simple option is to select one or more correct answers, while the answers may or may not change their location upon subsequent entry into the testing subsystem. Such test options allow you to identify a lack of knowledge in the section as a whole, since they basically contain questions that cover the entire course under study.
- Calculation and input or selection of the calculated value from the proposed options, which develops the students' ability to use electronic educational material—remember and correctly apply the necessary formulas and graphs.
- The construction a logical chain of answers, as well as a task with establishing compliance, which allows developing logical thinking, which is required in many situations in life, as well as in solving complex technical problems.
- The construction of flowcharts, as well as the preparation of true statements that allow developing flexibility and originality of thinking, ability to establish patterns.
- The construction of formulas from the source data, which develops the ability of students to memorize complex formulas (which will be useful in the further development of the course) and special attention, since it is necessary to draw up an expression in a clearly defined order, taking into account all the necessary signs: multiplication, division, summation, subtraction.
- Tests that combine several display options discussed above.

During the implementation of the testing subsystem, it is possible to record response times, while to simplify the task, it is possible to determine not the absolute time spent on the test, but the deviation from the average value both up and down, and also set the time limit for the test, which disciplines the learner in a certain degree. It is also necessary to take into account the number of incorrect answers and the types of tests in which these errors were made, and based on these results, display a report that reflects the time spent on the tests, the total number of questions asked, the number of incorrect answers, as well as the numbers (or text with the task) of those questions where errors were made. Such report is the basis for the formation of the functions (1), (2) and subsequent constructing an individual trajectory of the student, reflecting the gaps in his knowledge, as well as the peculiarities of the perception of the material being studied, which will allow to pay more attention to the re-study of exactly the educational section where mistakes were made. The report can be displayed on the screen (see Fig. 4), printed, or saved to a file.

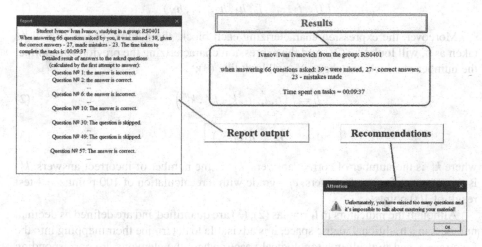

Fig. 4. Report of student's test completion

To form individual portraits of students, in addition to creating intellectual lectures, it is also necessary to have information about the successful delivery of previous disciplines that affect the study of this discipline. For this, a table should be formed with a list of previously studied courses (disciplines), which, according to the current standard, are preceding and influencing the study of this discipline. This table, which can be resized, shows the name of the previous course and the previous grade. Also, the table records the test results for these courses, which are held at the beginning of the study of this course at the first start. Grade for the course (discipline) is taken from the record books or other official bases. Ideally, it is generated automatically if there is an electronic document management system containing this information.

In the constructed intellectual lecture-presentation, one can conditionally distinguish two subsystems: training, consisting of slides with the studied educational material, and testing, containing various test tasks. As a result of this construction of a lecture-presentation, important information is accumulated about the student's educational trajectory, which, with appropriate analysis, can become not just a set of control indicators received by the teacher, but also an intellectual system that prompts the student for his further behavior in the form of certain recommendations, as well as reasonable restrictions and certain prohibitions.

Let us agree through t_i to denote the control time for passing the i-th block, shown in Fig. 1 by the dotted line, and through $t_i^{'}$ the time of real study by the student of this block. By $\tau_i = t_i - t_i^{'}$ we will denote the algebraic difference of times t_i and $t_i^{'}$ (the values $t_i, t_i^{'}$ and τ_i characterize each block, and in tests – each question). At the same time, the following indicators are added to each question: the number of incorrect answers to each question, the number of correct answers and the missing questions.

As a result, we have some functional that in general can be written as:

$$F(f_1, f_2, \ldots, f_n, h_1, h_2, \ldots, h_N) \tag{1}$$

Moreover, the expression characterizing each block, the number of which will be taken as n, will look like (2). And the expression characterizing the previous discipline, the number of which we take as N, will look like (3):

$$f_i = f\left(t_i, t_i^{'}, \tau_i, k_i^c, k_i^{ic}, k_i^m\right) \tag{2}$$

$$h_j = h(e_j, s_j) \tag{3}$$

where k_i^c is the number of correct answers, k_i^{ic} is the number of incorrect answers, k_i^m is the number of missed answers, e_j – grade with a recalculation of 100 points; s_j – test result of 100 points.

Although the indicators in formulas (2), (3) are quantified and are defined as decimal numbers in a traditional metric space, it is advisable to determine their mapping into the functions f_i and h_j itself in a topological space, where the elements are corresponding logical recommendations to the student to improve the study of the discipline. In addition, the indicators should form a student's educational portrait for the teacher, reflecting his personal achievements in the study of the corresponding discipline. General data on the student's trajectory and his portrait will be formed according to expression (1), which can ultimately serve as his corresponding assessment, according to the introduced measurement scale.

The totality of the collected time parameters in the teaching and testing subsystems, as well as the results of the testing itself, are analyzed to identify the dynamics of the course learning, as well as to develop appropriate instructions in the form of "Recommendations and useful tips" that may appear after any slide. Such instructions can be both advisory in nature, for example, to be more attentive to the study, and directive, compulsory, namely, to return to the initial slide from which the study of this section began in order to master the material again. Thus, the instructions "Recommendations and useful tips" included in the presentation accompany the studied course and is to attract the student's attention for a more careful study and assimilation of the proposed content. The aggregate of all data obtained as a result of training using an intelligent lecture-presentation with a built-in testing subsystem is accumulated and used for further control of the student's knowledge, as well as for the subsequent development of the student's individual educational trajectory and adjustment of the control time [11].

4   Conclusion

As a result, on the basis of the proposed model, an intelligent educational lecture-presentation was created on the discipline "Information Theory" with built-in tests, marked by the type of test, as well as with the definition of the section of the course to which this test belongs. The obtained data allow building individual trajectories for students, which allows them to master the studied discipline with greater efficiency, and the teacher - to receive objective data on the course of the educational process and, if necessary, correct it. At the same time, in order to create a full-fledged SMART-learning process, it is necessary to have such intelligent lectures that make it possible to build individual educational trajectories of students, both in the study of the material and in the control of knowledge (passing test tasks), in all studied disciplines, as well as a database indicating the studied disciplines and the grade obtained as a result of mastering these disciplines. In addition, the interaction of all these subsystems is necessary for the implementation of the ideas of SMART-learning in general. The creation of systems with IETS has a number of advantages, among which one can single out greater accessibility, dynamism, mobility, and in addition, the formation of a student's readiness for self-development and his adequate self-esteem.

References

1. Adzhemov, A.S., Manonina, I.V., Shestakov, V.V.: Features of smart learning at high school. Informat. Educ. **10**, 47–53 (2020)
2. Sinn, J.W.: Electronic course delivery in higher education: promise and challenge. J. Technol. Stud. **30**(1/2), 39–45 (2004)
3. Guerlac, S.: Humanities 2.0: E-learning in the digital world. Human. Crisis Public Univ. **116**(1), 102–127 (2011)
4. Federal Law of December 29, 2012 No. 273-FZ "On Education in the Russian Federation". https://docs.cntd.ru/document/902389617
5. Shaposhnikova, N.: Individual educational trajectory of a student: analysis of interpretations of the concept. Pedag. Educ. Russia **5**, 39–44 (2015)
6. Sysoev, P.: Teaching on an individual trajectory. Lang. Cult. **4**, 121–131 (2013)
7. Khutorskoy, A.V.: Personality-Oriented Learning Methodology. How Do You Teach Everyone Differently? Teacher's Manual. Vlados-Press Publishing House, Moscow (2005)
8. Kozimor-King, M.L., Chin, J.: Learning from Each Other: Refining the Practice of Teaching in Higher Education. University of California Press, Oakland (2018)
9. Adzhemov, A.S.: Features of the methodical presentation of lectures in the form of Microsoft Powerpoint-presentation on the example of the discipline BCT. Method. Issues Teach. Infocommun. Higher Educ. **6**(1), 4–6 (2017)
10. Gier, V.S., Kreiner, D.S.: Incorporating active learning with powerpoint-based lectures using content-based questions. Teach. Psychol. **36**(2), 134–139 (2009)
11. Adzhemov, A., Manonina, I., Shestakov, V.: General and custom solutions for the use of info-communication technologies in learning. In: Systems of Signal Synchronization, Generating and Processing in Telecommunications (SYNCHROINFO) 2018, pp. 1–5, IEEE (2018)

Application of an Adaptive Domain-Specific Interface in a Decision-Support System for Planning Railroad Technical Services

Boris Ulitin[✉] [iD], Eduard Babkin[iD], and Tatiana Babkina[iD]

HSE University, Nizhny Novgorod, Russia
{bulitin,eababkin,tbabkina}@hse.ru

Abstract. The use of intelligent systems with advanced AI algorithms is a key aspect of enterprise digitalization. The railway domain is not an exception. We argue, that the quality of any AI-based system greatly depends on the methods of computer-human interaction. We propose an approach to organize the interaction of the end user with the AI-based system through a domain-specific language with a specific feature – the language can continuously adapt to the new requirements of end users without the need to recreate the system as a whole. This allows not only to simplify the process of creating domain-specific interfaces, but also to make the process of making changes to the DSL and the corresponding AI-based system independent, but coordinated. Applicability of the approach is demonstrated using a real-life example of a resource allocation task in the railway transportation.

Keywords: Domain-specific language · UML · Transformation · Evolution · Invariants · Decision-support system · Planning technical service · Resource allocation problem

1 Introduction

During the decade the degree of autonomy of the enterprise components increases as well as the intensity of their interaction [2]. In these circumstances, the importance of artificial intelligence (AI) systems is growing [1]. Many cases demonstrate that AI-based systems properly and quickly respond by a fully automated manner to changes of the context of the problem being solved.

However, even in the case of complete automation, the need for user interaction with artificial intelligence remains [3]. First of all, such interaction is necessary for the accumulation of the knowledge base used by AI during its work. In addition, users may need various sorts of *ad hoc* analytical information from the AI-system. Finally, there are situations that are not foreseen in the algorithms of behavior for AI-system and require the direct control by the end-user.

The railway allocation problem, which includes scheduling and processing of trains, service brigades using station equipment, exemplifies the challenge of designing a proper interaction between operators and an AI-based system in dynamic contexts. One of the

E. Babkin et al. (Eds.): MOBA 2022, LNBIP 457, pp. 110–124, 2022.
https://doi.org/10.1007/978-3-031-17728-6_10

options for organizing interaction with such systems can be a domain-specific language (DSL). The main specificity of such a language is that it is based on the terms used in the subject area and, thus, is the most understandable for end users. From this point of view, DSL is based on the conceptual model of the subject area and corresponds to it as much as possible.

We also need to note that the sceneries of working with DSL may vary due to considerable differences in experience of information needs of different DSL users. As a result, in parallel to the development of the skills and knowledge of the user, the set of DSL terms, that he/she operates with, can also evolve.

To increase the efficiency and simplify interactions between operators and an AI-based system, it is necessary to develop new generic approaches, which enable continuous adaptation of user domain-based interfaces for actual conditions of human-machine interaction. Existing works [9, 11] pay more attention to automation of AI optimization algorithms rather than to processes of interaction with AI systems. In most works, and in particular in the works [10] by Konyrbaev et al., the user interface is developed immediately as full and general as possible and subsequently can only be changed manually. Such a statement deprives the user interface of possible flexibility and leads to cases when the user interface begins to contradict the conceptual model of the domain.

In previous works we substantiated that any interface can be interpreted as a kind of domain-specific language (DSL) [17], and an object-oriented paradigm naturally represents the interface, since it reflects elements of the conceptual model of the domain. Thus, when solving the problem of adapting an interface, models and methods common to the DSL approach can be applied. This leads us to the idea that the interface also has a model-oriented nature, which means that it is possible to automate the process of its incremental modification during the evolution of a conceptual domain model.

Within a generic framework of the DSL design that article aims at proposing a new approach to automation of development of adaptive domain-specific interfaces for decision support systems in the railway domain. In particular, we offer such adaptable interface for an AI-based decision support system which provides efficient planning of technical services. In our approach we use transformations between the UML-model and the ontology restrained by a certain invariant formalism. The UML-model describes the component structure of the user interface. In turn, the ontology is used as a conceptual model of the domain. Invariants represent stable structures, the correspondences between which are established at the level of both models [14, 15]. A certain transformation is used to shift between identified invariants of both models and to adapt the interface components to changes in the domain model. This approach allows us to reduce efforts during the interface designing. In addition, due to the formal model of invariants [14, 15], the interface structure can always be consistently adapted to changes in the domain model.

Our new contributions provide a reusable approach to continuous reconfiguration and adaptation of DSL in respond to changing conditions. In this paper, we focus more on adapting the graphical components of the DSL, namely, the interfaces. The application of the approach is considered by the example of adaptation of interfaces for a specialized multi-agent system for real-time scheduling technical services. This case was chosen because of a great impact on knowledge-based digitalization of railway companies.

However, the proposed approach is not limited to this system, but allows one to similarly supplement the adaptive interface with other intelligent systems in railway domain.

An additional result of the work on the approach includes a new domain ontology. The ontology developed fully describes the structure of the available resources of the railway station in the context of the process of their distribution and can be used by specialists and dispatchers to optimize the station processes.

This article describes our approach and presents results as follows. In Sect. 2 we observe main prerequisites and scientific foundations of representation of user interfaces by UML class-diagram and show correspondence between the UML class-diagram and the ontological model of the domain. We also introduce the concept of invariants, their classification and formalisms. Section 3 contains the description of the proposed approach, specifies the invariants of the domain model and the interface model and determines the transformations between them. Section 4 is devoted to the application of proposed approach for planning railway technical services. We conclude the article with the analysis of the proposed approach and further research steps.

2 Key Prerequisites and Concepts of the Research

2.1 The Decision Support System for Planning Technical Railway Services

The process of allocating resources of a railway station involves managing many different trains, tracks, service brigades and equipment. Due to frequent changes in the context of the problem and evolving users' experience classical approaches to solving the resource allocation problem become ineffective.

In this case, it seems expedient to use AI-based multi-agent approaches that are based on the representation of the problem being solved as a result of the interaction of various agents.

Recently such a multi-agent decision support system has been developed for solving resource allocations problem [19] where each resource of the railway station is represented as a separate agent with the corresponding characteristics (the current work represents for the ontological description of the domain in Sect. 4.1).

In the process of finding a solution, agents interact with each other, finding the best match among themselves. Agent-trains try to find for the most suitable agent-track along the length, as well as the agent-brigade in accordance with the required set of services. In the process of analyzing the decision, each agent uses a formal constraints-based model that helps to distribute arriving trains in time and protect them against time-conflicts. In more details this system of constraints was described in [19].

Within the framework of that decision support system in our present research we specifically consider an issue of human-machine interaction. Taking into account the dynamic context of the problem being solved, as well as the variety of agents involved in it, there is a need for a flexible and adaptable graphical interface (GUI). That interface should provide the ability to dynamically add to the underlying decision support system new types of resources (and equivalent agents) and their constraint model, assuming that the changes must occur in real time, without a chance to rebuild the system as a whole.

In such circumstances the interface to the decision support system should explicitly represent all available resources of the railway station in terms of so-called Domain

Semantic Model and use the paradigm of domain specific languages (DSL). In this case, a change in the interface can be made out as a result of the transformation of the conceptual model and obtained without re-creating the system as a whole.

2.2 Definition of Domain Semantic Model (DSM)

According to Parr [20] DSM offers a flexible and agile representation of domain knowledge. DSM can be constituted by either just small pieces of a domain knowledge (e.g. small taxonomies equipped with few rules) or rich and complex ontologies (obtained, for example, by translating existing ontologies). That gives respectively weak or rich and detailed representation of a domain [21]. More formally DSM is a seven-tuple of the form:

$$DSM = (\mathcal{H}_C, \mathcal{H}_R, O, R, A, M, D) \tag{1}$$

The DSM above can be separated into three interconnected layers: the meta-layer ($\mathcal{H}_C$ and $\mathcal{H}_R$) with sets of classes and relations schemas, which identifies the way to define the DSL itself; the object-layer (O and R) with objects and tuples, which represent the main concepts in the target domain and relations between them and the logical layer (A, D and M) with axioms, descriptors and reasoning modules, which postulates the rules, existing in the target domain and different restrictions on them. In practice, all these layers are important and have to be considered during the effective DSL development. However, based on the DSL definition, we are interested mostly in the object-layer of DSL, which consists of the objects and relations between them, which form the basis of the future DSL. In what follows, we will be focused on this object-layer of DSM.

It is also important to note, that DSM usually has a dynamic structure, demonstrates a tendency to changes over the time (evolution, in other words). With the evolution of the domain, the evolution of its DSM also occurs. As a result, any DSL, based on the corresponding DSM, should be adopted according to the changes. Consequently, the structure of the DSL metamodel should be as close as possible to the structure of DSM in order to guarantee the coherence between DSL and the target domain. So, that is reasonable to select a common meta-meta model which will be used both for definition of a DSL metamodel and DSM. We believe that a widely accepted object-oriented meta-meta model can be suitable for our purposes. The following manifestation of DSL as a special kind of the object-oriented model proves that believe.

2.3 Object-Oriented Definition of DSL

From the point of view of the end user, the DSL is a set of objects and operations on them. Interfaces are used to interact with DSL objects, which results in the idea that each DSL object has an equivalent at the interface level. As a result, the interface is a kind of reflection of the structure of the DSL and can be considered as a special type of DSL. This means that general approaches to organizing the adaptation of interfaces are applicable for organizing the evolution of DSL and vice versa.

Object-oriented representation of the Graphical user interface (GUI) in general settles as a part of the object-oriented analysis and design (OOAD) approach [4]. It's a structured method for analyzing, designing a system by applying the object-orientated concepts, and develop a set of graphical system models during the development life cycle of the software [4].

The main goal of this modular approach is to break down the system into smaller units, called objects, that can stand on their own and be changed without affecting the ones around them too much. From this point of view, any system is represented as a set of interconnected components (objects), characterized by their attributes and behavior.

According to this idea, we separate the system into *objects*, each of which has

- an identity (id) which distinguishes it from other objects in the system;
- a state that determines the attributes of an object as well as attributes' values;
- behavior that represents available activities performed by an object in terms of changes in its state.

Objects containing the same attributes and/or exhibit common behavior organize *classes*, which contain a set of attributes for the objects that are to be instantiated from the class and operations that portray the behavior of the objects of the class.

Therefore, we can formalize any class as a combination (O, R) of some objects and relations between them, where each object is a set of its attributes (one of attributes is unique and is considered an identifier) and operations $o_i = (Attr_i, Opp_i) = (\{attr_{i_1}, attr_{i_2}, \ldots, attr_{i_M}\}, \{opp_{i_1}, opp_{i_2}, \ldots, opp_{i_K}\}), M, K \in \mathbb{N}, i = 1, N)$.

Thus, the system is represented as a superposition of many objects of various classes. Being an integral part of the system, GUI can also be represented as a combination of the number of related objects of various classes. It is important to note that attributes may be elementary or complex [4]. Complex is an attribute that is an instance of a class (object). Elementary is an attribute containing a constant value that is not an object. Given this classification of attributes, we can argue that the system is a hierarchy of interconnected objects. At the lower level of such a hierarchy there are objects containing only elementary attributes, and at the top - the system itself. Such basic lower level objects that cannot be dissected into smaller components, make up system object invariants. Such object invariants make it possible to describe the structure as a superposition of low-level invariants. Functionals used to construct structures from object invariants form an operational invariant. These types of invariants are described in more detail in Sect. 2.4.

In this case, each object and, as a consequence, the GUI represents a combination of many object invariants that do not change and can be used to automate the development process. Assuming that the GUI is tied to a certain data set, we can identify the invariants at the DSM level as well as at the level of the GUI. As a result, the construction of the GUI becomes nothing else than the identification of the invariant at the DSM level with the subsequent search and display of its equivalent at the interface level.

Any change in the interface can be interpreted as a result of evolution. Taking into account, that any component of the interface is a combination (O, R), the evolution of the interface is a process of changes in the structure of its model.

The very problem in these circumstances is to prove, that one interface model is the result of evolution of another. In a simple way, it means, that one interface model can be derived during the transformation of another. Thus, both models contain a set of the same objects (components) and/or relations between them, which are identified as invariants for these models.

Most importantly, such invariants can be distinguished in the implementation of any type of evolution (both vertical and horizontal) [22]. The only difference is that in the case of vertical evolution, new components are added to the interface, and in the horizontal, the level of detail of existing ones changes.

From a structural point of view, all these changes are carried out with objects and relations between them. This unification of evolution through the allocation of minimal components in the interface allows you to automate the process of its development. In more detail, the mechanisms for determining invariants in model transformations were analyzed in our previous paper [18]. Here we use only the main points regarding the object transformations of models among themselves.

2.4 Definition and Classification of Invariants

There are at least 4 options for determining invariants depending on the context of use. This paper uses two classic forms of invariants: object-oriented (object) and inductive [14, 15].

Declarations of *object invariants* can appear in every class. The invariants that pertain to an object o are those declared in the classes between *object* – the root of the single-inheritance hierarchy – and *type*(o) – the allocated type of o. Each object o has a special field *inv*, whose value names a class in the range from *object* to *type*(o), and which represents the most refined subclass whose invariant can be relied upon for this object. More precisely, for any object o and class T and in any execution state of the program, if $o.inv$ is a subclass of T, which we denote by $o.inv \leq T$, then all object invariants declared in class T are known to hold for o. The object invariants declared in other classes may or may not hold for o, so they cannot be relied upon.

Inductive invariants describe the connection between components of two (or more) sets of objects and are denoted with inv_τ. For this type of invariants two types of specifications are defined, *next* and *inv*:

$$next_\tau.(p, q).F \triangleq [p \Rightarrow \mathcal{W}.F.q] inv_\tau.p.F \triangleq next_\tau.(p, p).F \wedge [\mathcal{J}.F \Rightarrow p] \quad (2)$$

Informally, $next_\tau.(p, q)$ means that whenever a transition is fired from a state that satisfies p, the resulting state satisfies q. Similarly, $inv_\tau.p$ specifies that p is true in any initial state and is preserved by every atomic transition. Therefore, by induction, p is true in every state. It should be noted that, since $[\mathcal{W}.F.q \Rightarrow q]$ because of possible stuttering $next_\tau.(p, q).F \Rightarrow [p \Rightarrow q]$.

According to that definition, an inductive invariant means, that there is a strong correspondence between elements of two sets of objects, which are connected during some relation (transformation). Given the formalisms above we aim to determine the invariants at the level of the DSM and interface and establish a correspondence between them. Our contributions will be described in the next section.

3 Description of the Approach Proposed

The core of our approach formalizes the transformation between UML Class diagram and the DSM in the form of invariants. For this purpose, we use two types of previously reviewed invariants: object and inductive. First of all, we reveal object invariants at the level of the DSM and the interface. Then, we define a function that will analyze the invariants in the DSM and find the corresponding interface-level invariant for them. Such invariant is added to the set of previously found interface components and is displayed on the screen.

We argue that in the case of an interface, the invariant will be expressed in the form of classes, which describe its individual components and do not contain references to other classes.

From this point of view, we represent each interface object as a class $C = (id, C, SA, CA, MA, O, R)$, where: id is the name assigned to the class; C is a finite set of classes due to a class can be composed of other classes; SA, CA, MA are finite sets of single, composed and multi-valued attributes correspondingly; Op is a finite set of operations and Rel is a finite set of relationships where the class is participating [12].

In the case of the DSM, the invariants are objects and their attributes, which are fully consistent with class attributes. These objects are object invariants.

Since an association class is both an association and a class, the mapping function is like the one defined for a class plus the references to the classes to which the association class is linked: $f : AC = (id, Ref(C_1), Ref(C_2), \ldots, Ref(C_n), SA, CA, MA, Op) \rightarrow T = ('name', Ref(C_1), Ref(C_2), \ldots, Ref(C_n), BIT, RT, AT, T, MM)$ where the T defined for the association class contains the references to the classes related by the association plus the built-in (BIT) data types, row types, array types, Ts, and member methods of the association class. Using this function, we can design the interface based on the DSM in the form of a complete invariant scheme.

Sequential application of the transformation function fully defines the interface development process. At the same time application of inductive invariants allows us to state that the final state of the interface will fully correspond to the DSM. Combination of these results provides the ability to automate the process of developing interfaces and their adaptation in the case of a change in the structure of DSM objects, since it is tied not to the structure as a whole, but to separated invariants.

Finally, we can formulate the following algorithm for DSL evolution:

1. Identify the original state of the DSL model M1.
2. Identify the final state of the DSL model M2.
3. Identify the object invariants between M1 and M2 in order to guarantee their consistency.
4. Apply the equivalent transformations to object invariants.
5. Describe the transformations for objects and functions, not presented in the object invariants.

This algorithm provides the opportunity to organize any type of DSL evolution, since it was shown, that any DSL evolution contains invariants at different levels of the structure of the model that describes the corresponding level of DSL.

4   Application of the Approach

Using the approach proposed we have a clear and simple way to continuously adapt the DSL-based user interface of the decision support system described (Sect. 2.1), responsible for finding the optimal resource allocation in the railway domain.

4.1   Formal Description of the Domain Using Ontologies

According to our approach in the process of DSL design, it's vital to identify all the types of resources in this domain.

In the current research, we use the ontology to represent all the resources of the railway station. A fragment of the application ontology of this domain is represented in Fig. 1 in the form of a generic semantic network, whose vertices are basic concepts, and arcs express relations between them (part-whole, gender-type, reservation, etc.).

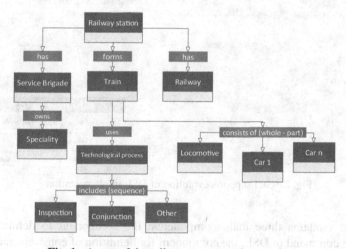

Fig. 1. A part of the railway transportation ontology

All resources for any railway station are represented in the DSM for the corresponding domain, which is more complete in comparison with that considered in our previous work [19], since it contains the specification of the requirements (Skills) both for the Services and for the Brigades providing them.

After the DSM created, we can identify the semantic level of DSL, describing the DSL meta-model. For this purpose, M2M transformation rules can be used, as it was described in [17]. In addition, M2M transformations are independent from the notation of model definition, that allows us to describe DSM and DSL meta-model independently, in the most appropriate way.

As a result, we will have the complete DSL metamodel, which can be used during the following DSL syntax definition. This definition includes two parts: definition of objects for DSL syntax, which are the equivalents to the objects, described on the semantic level of DSL, and grammar, describing the operations and correct terms for the future DSL syntax. In our case, we used the Backus-Naur form of grammar definition, because this form allows us to identify rules, based on the previously created objects, and automatically convert the resulting rules into an abstract, language-independent form.

The semantic and syntactic levels of DSL are wholly coherent and can be evolved using transformations in real time. In addition, such changes are provided separately, since the invariants on both levels are identified.

4.2   A Scenario of Adaptation of the Domain-Specific Interface

As it was mentioned before, the interface created contains two parts: the first one, responsible for the DSL scenario definition and processing, and another one, needed for evolution of DSL. The first part was described in detail and analyzed in [19], therefore, here we focus on the second part, which provides the evolution of DSL (Fig. 2).

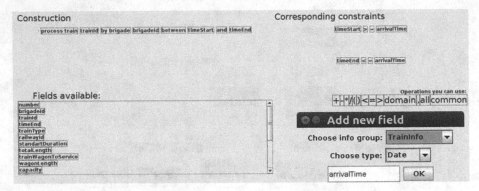

Fig. 2. GUI supports evolution of DSL implementation

This part contains three main components: the component to define/change a new/existing command of DSL, the component for definition of constraints, connected with the command and the component for definition of syntactic terms, related to the new command. All these components are identified in accordance with the structure of DSL: objects, which contain attributes and operations and relations between them. As a result, the created interface allows us to define the whole DSL structure and change it in real time without need to re-create the DSL manually.

Furthermore, this tool allows you to transfer the changes made to the DSM, thereby ensuring its full consistency with the updated interface structure. This is achieved due to the fact that in the interface we define the object invariants (attributes of objects) defined in both models. Such an invariant structure of changes makes it possible to organize in a universal way both vertical and horizontal evolution of DSL.

For example, we can extend syntactic part of DSL by adding new command: *process train trainId by brigade brigadeId from timeStart till timeEnd*. This command uses existing objects for the DSL semantic level: a train and a brigade, but implements a new syntactic term. In order to implement this command, the user should define a needed command, using the block of available fields of DSL objects. As a result, the following construction is defined (Fig. 2). After the term definition, constraints, related to this, are defined. Finally, the created term is compiled and added to the DSL, ready to use.

Using this interface, other sceneries of DSL evolution can also be implemented. For example, it is possible to create new groups of objects (Fig. 3).

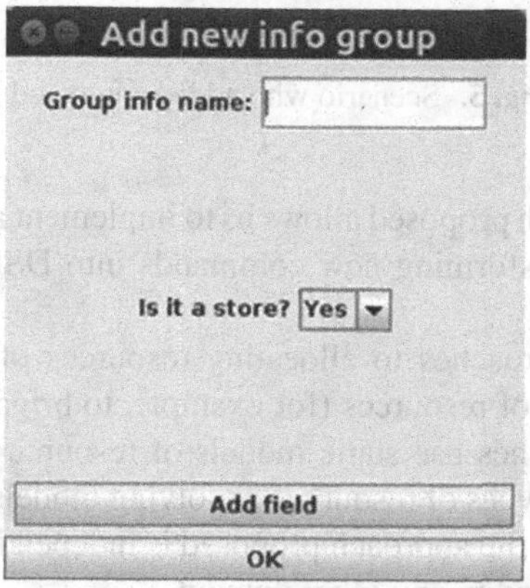

Fig. 3. Interface for creating new groups of objects

Similar to adding a new command, the user first of all must specify the name of the group being created, and also determine whether it is a repository (a group that combines information on the key fields of several other objects). Then it is necessary to specify the necessary fields of the group created (Add field), defining their names and type (domain). For example, we can add a new attribute *arrivalTime* to the *TrainInfo* object. For this purpose, the corresponding interface component can be used (Fig. 2), or add a new attribute to *WagonInfo* (Fig. 4).

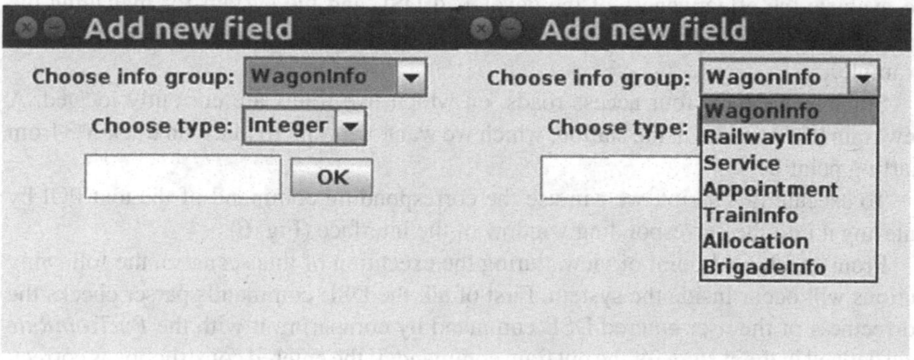

Fig. 4. Interface for adding a new field to a group

What is the most important, in this case, we only define new commands, without need to re-create the DSL structure and can use them in sceneries in real time. For example, the result of added command is represented in Fig. 5.

Fig. 5. Scenario with added command

As follows, the approach proposed allows us to implement all types of DSL evolution in real time, correctly transforming new commands into DSL syntactic and semantic objects and terms.

Currently existing approaches to allocating resources of railway station, are targeted to one concrete type of resources (for example, to brigades by Wang et al. [23]). Furthermore, such approaches use static models of resource allocation and cannot be adopted according to new types of resources or solving models in real time. In comparison to existing approaches, the approach proposed is independent from the nature of the resources and can be adopted to any other domain.

The only limitation for our approach is the fact, that the framework represented can provide the opportunity to define only unidirectional transformation of DSL, according to changes in the domain model. This limitation can be explained by the fact, that languages of model transformations do not support bidirectional transformations, because symmetric transformation means using the opposite to the original operation (delete instead of add, etc.). However, such limitation can be resolved using the idea of closure operations necessary for organizing the DSL evolution [18].

4.3 A User-Case for Evaluating the Effectiveness of the System

To evaluate the effectiveness of the developed DSL and the system for managing the resources of a railway station, we will consider its use during several scenarios as an example.

Suppose we have four access roads, on which five trains are currently located. A new train (№6) arrives at the station, which we want, we want to place on track №3 from starting point 21.

To execute this script, we can use the corresponding command of the text POI by entering it into the corresponding window of the interface (Fig. 6).

From a technical point of view, during the execution of this scenario, the following actions will occur inside the system. First of all, the DSL commands parser checks the correctness of the user-entered DSL command by comparing it with the *PutTrainRule* rule defined in the system for the put train command. If the entered construction is correct, the data from it will be supplemented with constraints read from the *PutTrainRule* using java reflection tools, and a table of constraints for the solver will be generated. Finally, the constructed table of constraints is sent to the solver, which tries to find a solution (the distribution of compositions between paths) taking into account the refined context of the problem.

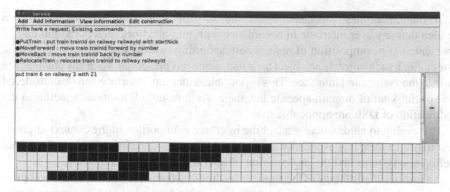

Fig. 6. Scenario PutTrain

In this case, the solution is found, so it is fixed and displayed on the corresponding panel of the visual DSL (interface), as shown in Fig. 7.

Similarly, the user can create other scenarios using the appropriate GUI components.

Thus, we see that the service built on the basis of DSL fully satisfies the requirement for the implementation of a coordinated and automated evolution of DSL. Furthermore, both horizontal and vertical evolution are available to the user. This does not require the re-creation of the entire system and the DSL, since all changes are carried out consistently in real time.

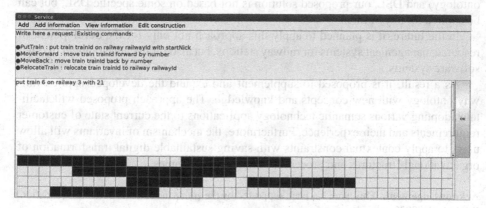

Fig. 7. Result of the scenario PutTrain

5   Conclusion

This article examines the process of automatically build interfaces based on a conceptual domain model by introducing invariant mechanisms. The motivation in the analysis of this process is based on the fact that various corporate systems use artificial intelligence systems, which require a convenient and flexible tool to interact with. In addition, in the process of evolution of end-user skills, interaction with the system may take on more complex forms and require modification of the interaction interfaces.

To implement these mechanisms, the authors propose an approach that is based on the idea that any user interface in accordance with an object-oriented paradigm can be represented as a composition of objects corresponding to individual components of the system. Each such object is an object invariant, since it is preserved when any changes are made to the system and interface. This is possible, since any interface can be considered as a special kind of domain-specific language. As a result, all methods specific to the modification of DSL are applicable to it.

This ability to automatically adapt the interface is important in the context of enterprise digitalization. It is especially important in the case of the introduction of artificial intelligence systems and the organization of interaction with the end user [3].

An additional advantage of the approach is the development of a complete ontological domain model, which combines not only the objects and the relationships between them, but also reflects the knowledge of end users.

As a result, the need to manually create an interface disappears, since it is built as a composition of individual invariants in real time. Such automation is achieved due to the fact that the interface is constructed as a superposition of object invariants. As a result, the interface structure is dynamically built in real time based on the DSM.

In comparison to existing solutions (like [23]), our approach allows users not only to specify the concrete DSL terms without opportunity to redefine them automatically in real time, but also to edit existing DSM and the whole DSL structure without recreating them according to changes both in the domain and competences of end-users. Furthermore, in contrast to using the graph-transformations for conversions between DSM (the ontology) and DSL, our proposed solution is not based on some specific DSL, but can be applied for any of them.

In the future, it is planned to apply this approach not only for the development of resource management systems for railway stations, but also for the development of other software systems.

As a result, it is proposed to supplement and expand the developed applied railway ontology with new concepts and knowledge. The approach proposed will facilitate adopting various semantic technology applications to the current state of customer requirements and their experience. Furthermore, the mechanism of invariants will allow users to apply contextual constraints with saving sustainable digital transformation of organizational structures and processes of modern companies.

Acknowledgement. This work has been supported by the grants the Russian Science Foundation, RSF 22-71-00032.

References

1. Nonaka, I., Kodama, M., Hirose, A., Kohlbacher, F.: Dynamic fractal organizations for promoting knowledge-based transformation – a new paradigm for organizational theory. Eur. Manag. J. **32**(1), 137–146 (2014)
2. Heavin, C., Power, D.J.: Challenges for digital transformation – towards a conceptual decision support guide for managers. J. Decis. Syst. **27**(1), 38–45 (2018)

3. Ruffolo, M., Sidhu, I., Guadagno, L.: Semantic enterprise technologies. In: Proceedings of the First International Conference on Industrial Results of Semantic Technologies, vol. 293, pp. 70–84 (2007)

4. Hayat, S.A.E., Toufik, F., Bahaj, M.: UML/OCL based design and the transition towards temporal object relational database with Bitemporal data. J. King Saud Univ. Comput. Inf. Sci. **32**(4), 398–407 (2020)

5. Bashir, R.S., Lee, S.P., Khan, S.U.R., Chang, V., Farid, S.: UML models consistency management: Guidelines for software quality manager. Int. J. Inf. Manag. **36**(6), 883–899 (2016)

6. Lazareva, O.F., McInnerney, J., Williams, T.: Implicit relational learning in a multiple-object tracking task. Behav. Process. **152**, 26–36 (2018)

7. Wu, Y., Mu, T., Liatsis, P., Goulermas, J.Y.: Computation of heterogeneous object co-embeddings from relational measurements. Pattern Recogn. **65**, 146–163 (2017)

8. Torres, A., Galante, R., Pimenta, M.S., Martins, A.J.B.: Twenty years of object-relational mapping: a survey on patterns, solutions, and their implications on application design. Inf. Softw. Technol. **82**, 1–18 (2017)

9. Wang, N., Wang, D., Zhang, Y.: Design of an adaptive examination system based on artificial intelligence recognition model. Mech. Syst. Signal Process. **142**, 1–14 (2020)

10. Konyrbaev, N.B., Ibadulla, S.I., Diveev, A.I.: Evolutionary methods for creating artificial intelligence of robotic technical systems. Procedia Comput. Sci. **150**, 709–715 (2019)

11. Leung, Y.: Artificial intelligence and expert systems. In: International Encyclopedia of Human Geography, 2nd edn. pp. 209–215. Elsevier (2020)

12. Golobisky, M.F., Vecchietti, A.: Mapping UML class diagrams into object-relational schemas. In: Proceedings of Argentine Symposium on Software Engineering, pp. 65–79 (2005)

13. Köhler, H., Link, S.: SQL schema design: foundations, normal forms, and normalization. Inf. Syst. **76**, 88–113 (2018)

14. Chen, Y., Tang, Z.: Vector invariant fields of finite classical groups. J. Algebra **534**, 129–144 (2019)

15. Carvalho, J.F., Pequito, S., Aguiar, A.P., Kar, S., Johansson, K.H.: Composability and controllability of structural linear time-invariant systems: distributed verification. Automatica **78**, 123–134 (2017)

16. SQL Standart 2016 (ISO/IEC 9075-1:2016). https://www.iso.org/committee/45342/x/catalogue/p/1/u/0/w/0/d/0

17. Ulitin, B., Babkin, E., Babkina, T.: A projection-based approach for development of domain-specific languages. In: Zdravkovic, J., Grabis, J., Nurcan, S., Stirna, J. (eds.) BIR 2018. LNBIP, vol. 330, pp. 219–234. Springer, Cham (2018). https://doi.org/10.1007/978-3-319-99951-7_15

18. Ulitin, B., Babkin, E., Babkina, T., Vizgunov, A.: Automated formal verification of model transformations using the invariants mechanism. In: Pańkowska, M., Sandkuhl, K. (eds.) BIR 2019. LNBIP, vol. 365, pp. 59–73. Springer, Cham (2019). https://doi.org/10.1007/978-3-030-31143-8_5

19. Ulitin, B., Babkin, E.: Ontology-based reconfigurable DSL for planning technical services. IFAC-PapersOnLine **52**(13), 1138–1144 (2019)

20. Terence, P.: Language Implementation Patterns: Create Your Own Domain-Specific and General Programming Languages. Pragmatic Bookshelf (2012)

21. Haav, H.-M., Ojamaa, A., Grigorenko, P., Kotkas, V.: Ontology-based integration of software artefacts for DSL development. In: Ciuciu, I., et al. (eds.) OTM 2015. LNCS, vol. 9416, pp. 309–318. Springer, Cham (2015). https://doi.org/10.1007/978-3-319-26138-6_34

22. Cleenewerck, T.: Component-based DSL development. In: Pfenning, F., Smaragdakis, Y. (eds.) GPCE 2003. LNCS, vol. 2830, pp. 245–264. Springer, Heidelberg (2003). https://doi.org/10.1007/978-3-540-39815-8_15
23. Wang, H., Wang, X., Zhang, X.: Dynamic resource allocation for intermodal freight transportation with network effects: approximations and algorithms. Transp. Res. Part B: Methodol. **99**, 83–112 (2017)

Invited Paper

IT Crisisology: New Discipline for Business Agility

Sergey V. Zykov[1,2]([envelope]) [ORCID]

[1] National Research University Higher School of Economics, 20 Myasnitskaya Street,
Moscow 101000, Russian Federation
szykov@hse.ru

[2] MEPhI National Research Nuclear University, 31 Kashirskoe Shosse, Moscow 115409,
Russian Federation

Abstract. This paper examines crises in digital software production. It defines a
digital product development crisis and introduces IT Crisisology, the emerging discipline that systematically addresses such crises. The key I Crisisology ingredients
incorporate models, methods, tools, patterns, and best practices. The IT Crisisology framework deals with technology, business and human factors; for each kind of
these, it uses a custom-tailored set of the above ingredients. Their instances include
tradeoff optimization, agility matrix, models for knowledge transfer and data lifecycle. These ingredients are further enhanced and improved for enterprise-scale
development. Systemic application of the IT Crisisology framework promotes better disciplined, predictable, and manageable software product development, even
in a crisis.

Keywords: IT Crisisology · Software product development · Lifecycle
management · Agile methodology

1 Introduction

Crisis is an imbalance between the expectations of clients and the exact behaviour of the
product. It was due to rapid increases in computer power and the complexity of unhandled
problems. The term "crisis" is used in computer science to describe difficulties of writing
useful and efficient computer programs in a scheduled time. Let us define crisis in
software production as a situation of either premature project termination or insufficient
quality/late product delivery due to imbalance of project resources & product constraints.

Let us define IT Crisisology as a discipline that studies crises in software production,
including their monitoring, forecasting, detection, mitigation, resolution, resilient and
adaptive (either proactive or reactive) responding, and prevention. Crises affect both software project and software product. In software projects, crises occur in the form of over
budgeting, late delivery of projects, unmanageable projects whereas in software products they manifest themselves as the products being inefficient, low quality, essentially
different from customer requirements, difficult to maintain, and even undelivered.

© The Author(s), under exclusive license to Springer Nature Switzerland AG 2022
E. Babkin et al. (Eds.): MOBA 2022, LNBIP 457, pp. 127–138, 2022.
https://doi.org/10.1007/978-3-031-17728-6_11

2   IT Crisisology: Dimensions or "Pillars"

The first "pillar" refers to technical requirements (Fig. 1); these include quality attributes (portability, security, performance) and system-level framework such as integrated development environment (IDE), database management system (DBMS), and programming language (PL). The second "pillar" refers to business constrains; this occurs in the form of project delimiters (i.e. budgets, time to market) as well as the problem domain in which this crisis occurs. The third "pillar" is known as the human factor; this encapsulates such communication attributes as teambuilding ability, negotiation skills and the ability to transfer knowledge to other people. Let us refer to these "pillars" as the technology, business and human factors, i.e. "T"-factor, "B"-factor and "H"-factor. The idea is that removing any of the above "pillars" results in a "global" crisis (as it would with removing any leg of a three-legged stool), whereas neglecting any of these results in a "local" crisis due to their imbalance.

Fig. 1. The three "pillars" of IT Crisisology

3   Crises: The Ancient Myths

In April 12, 1959, the US President J.F. Kennedy said that a "crisis" meant an "opportunity" [20]; however, the Chinese word for crisis is typically composed of these two characters: "danger" and "situation" [9, 15, 16]. Notably, at this point of time the "Crisisology" was born as a phenomenon. As the years went by, researchers argued whether the crisis in Software Engineering is over or it still exists. In 2008, Coliburn et al., argued to prove that there was no software engineering crisis [2, 5]. However, in 2006, Buettner et al., argued conversely, stating that software engineering was indeed in a crisis [4]. All these happened, because of the fundamental differences in the lifecycles of software and material products, and due to human factor dependencies.

4   IT Crisisology: The Framework

This paper presents IT Crisisology, the discipline that systematically studies IT crises phenomena and their management [19]. This discipline addresses business, technical and human factors; it applies a carefully selected blend of the software engineering models, methods and tools that result in manageable (i.e. measured and predictable) projects, better quality products, conquering product complexity, ambiguity, and managing project uncertainty.

IT product management differs from financial management and material production management in many ways, some of which are its product type, which is up to 100% non-material, and its lifecycle (i.e. implementation and maintenance cost) [10]. The other key reason is communication ambiguity, as the developer and the client sides typically speak in difference languages. This is evident even from the Google search results, which report 612M for the "Crisis management" query [19], 629M for "Financial crisology" and 1.2K for "IT crisisolgy".

In 1968, the NATO organized the first conference in software engineering in Garmisch, Germany, in order to find a solution to what became known as "crisis" at that time [13]. Among the key delegates of this conference were Friedrich Bauer, Alan Perils, Edger Djikstra and Peter Naur. However, software has been in crisis for over 50 years. A number of models were developed due to the crisis; one example is the triangle crisis triangle (Fig. 3) based on the "Iron" (project) triangle (Fig. 2). Let us mention the "Quality", which, as a derivate of the "3D", deals with adjusting tradeoff and managing the project budget, project scope and project schedule.

The "crisis triangle consists of three zones. These include the "comfort" (i.e. green) zone, where there is little need for management since the actions proceed as planned, and this guarantees quality deliverables. The other zone is the "tradeoff" (i.e. yellow) zone, where a number of factor may be adjusted, and immediate actions are required in other to guarantee the quality. The third zone is the "crisis" (i.e. Red) zone; in this critical area, immediate actions are required to produce even a negotiable quality.

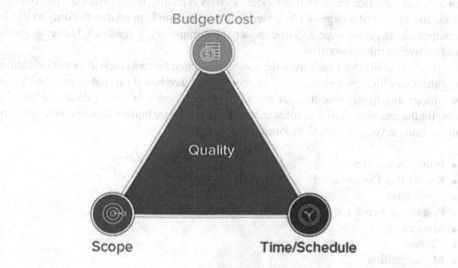

Fig. 2. The "iron" (project) triangle

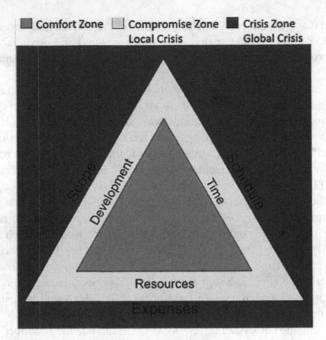

Fig. 3. The "crisis" triangle

Dealing with this crisis triangle, a paramount factor is the communication between the developer and the customer. Shannon information theory fits the "developer-and-customer" system, where the key issue is transferring messages without loss, especially in a "noisy" environment. In this model, a crisis typically results from an information loss, and in case of a large- scale system, such a loss can happen due to complexity. To compensate negative issue and to conquer the complexity, a feedback (either negative or positive) is mission-critical.

The soft skills that result from the so-called human factors (such as communication, negation, conflict management and teambuilding), are based on that is psychology or sociology and highly essential for the software engineers; however, these are initially rare for the technical staff (i.e. software developers). These human factors can be broken-down into "seven principles" of knowledge transfer:

- Prior Knowledge
- Knowledge Organization
- Motivation
- Practice + Feedback
- Mastery
- Climate
- Metacognition

Surprisingly, the human factors result in crises more often than the technical factors. In order to manage these, metrics to determine if the product development goals are met, how to achieve these goals and what is required, why the goals are necessary, time, priority and due date for each deliverable are established. These ingredients, taken together, are often referred to as SMART communication. Also, adaptive development practices such as teambuilding, Myers Briggs personality psychological types, Situation leadership model and Personal development model are considered [2].

This difference between developers and customers inspires the need for trade-off-based architecture (ACDM/ATAM). ACDM/ATAM reduces uncertainty and helps avoid crisis. How this model ensues that crisis is avoided by reducing uncertainly (Fig. 4). ACDM defines the main stages of work on the coordination of design and rapid, adaptive development of high-quality architectural design [18]. It helps teams to analyze, identify, and build architecture "drivers" in the early stages of software development. The architecture "drivers" help to design, evaluate and test a software development project. The results of the project evaluation contribute to the refinement of the architectural design. The ACDM method includes these three main components:

- Processes: these involve iterative development and clarification of th the architectural project
- Project evaluation: this determines whether the project is ready for production and identifies problems important to architecture.
- Architectural testing: this solves technical problems identified during the assessment, serves the or the refinement of the project, and requires (re)assessment until the product is ready for production

In ACDM, the main goal is software design. This is achieved by performing these tasks: identifying, analyzing and organizing architectural drivers, architectural project management and its documenting, project evaluation, management, iterative refinement of software design to reduce risk, assessment, planning and correction of the system/product at the level of architecture.

5 Agility: A Mission-Critical Crisisology Component

This is a set of approaches based on iterative development, where requirements and solutions evolve through the collaborative effort of teams and their customers, or end-users. It provides a response, which is rapid and flexible to the change like the crisis.

The general Agile software development lifecycle includes such phases as: Plan, Requirements Analysis, Design, Development, Test and Deployment. A number of software development methodologies follow the Agile way [3]. These include: Scrum, Extreme Programming (XP), Feature-driven Development (FDD), Adaptive Software Development (ASD), Lean Software Development (LSD), Kanban, Dynamic Software Development Method (DSDM), and Crystal Clear [6, 9, 11].

Agile methodologies help crisis management by employing the following techniques and practices:

- Continuous improvement: feedback from the system, the customer, and team members throughout the project. The aim is to improve future iterations using past records.

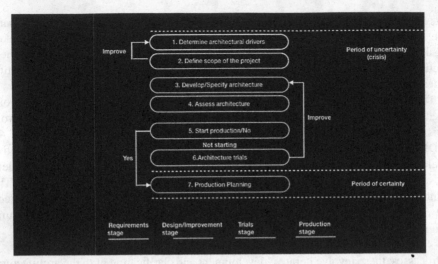

Fig. 4. ACDM/ATAM: SW development lifecycle

- Customers are informed and work closely with the team. Customers see the deliverables, share the input, and have an impact on the end product. The aim is to meet customer requirements.
- Changes: it is easy to accept and set changes with a shorter planning cycle. The aim is to refine and reprioritize items.
- Fast and high-quality project delivery: the product is broken down into manageable units. Team focus is high-quality development and testing. Bugs and errors identified and solved quickly; the product is delivered fast, with a reasonable schedule and budget.
- Team interaction: frequent and face-to-face communication results in high quality product.
- Continuous goal clarification: with a clear goal, development adapts to evolving requirements as project progresses within scope

6 Large-Scale Organizations: Managing the Lifecycles

In general, the lifecycle management in enterprises is similar to a person's life in a number of aspects [1]. The organization is born in creative and entrepreneurial agony experiencing the difficulties and joys of adolescence. It reaches maturity, and then many organizations begin to grow old and decline as young and dynamic competitors gradually replace them. The old age is usually followed by organizational death.

However, unlike people's lives, the lifecycle of organization is not limited to a certain time period. Examples of organizations are known that have been in their blossoming and maturity for decades; this can be observed in companies like Google, Apple and Amazon.

7 Large-Scale Organizations: Managing the Changes

Often, a problem or an opportunity created by a change, leads to a solution that will cause an even greater change, and as a result the customers face a new reality with a new set of problems or opportunities. When the systems change, they collapse and disintegrate. However, in order to break up and disintegrate, it is not necessary to be old. Just as young people sometimes commit suicide, young systems can also disintegrate [2]. Therefore, regardless of the age of the system, the cause of its disintegration is change, and the faster the change, the faster the disintegration that manifests itself in what we call problems. The lifecycle of an enterprise proceeds in a number of stages, which are summarized below.

The Courtship phase precedes the emergence of an organization that has not yet come into being and exists only as an idea. During the Courtship, the emphasis is typically o the ideas and opportunities that the future promises. The potential founder of the company experiences a burst of enthusiasm and willingly tells everyone about how wonderful his or her idea is.

The Infancy phase of the development of the organization is not important to what someone does rather than he or she thinks. The question that the founders must answer and which they ask their employees, looks like this: "What did you do? Did you manage to sell something, produce it, or bring it to an end?" Infant companies face an amazing paradox. The higher their risks, the higher their loyalty should be in order to ensure the achievement of success. At this phase of courtship, the founders must be dreamers capable of developing devotion to their dreams. However, as soon as a company enters the period of Infancy, the risk increases and it begins to demand persistent, result-oriented founders who are no longer dreamers.

The "Let's Go" phase is a dramatic period of abrupt transition from love to hatred. Workers may not like their leaders, but they continue to fear and respect them. If a company falls into the trap of the founder, it means that when the founder dies, the company dies.

In order for the company to be able to save the hard-earned wealth, it must move from management based on intuition and position (used in the "Come-Come" phase) to a more professional management. This process is carried out at the stage of the company's Youth. If the company does not implement such a transition, it falls into the founder's trap or into a family trap.

The Youth phase is characterized by a number of problems, such as: (i) a conflict between partners or decision-makers, (ii) a temporal loss of vision, (iii) unsystematic way of delegation of authority; therefore, the rules are established but not observed. The other problems that occur include: (i) inadequacy of goals, (ii) suspension of the founder, and (iii) rapid weakening of mutual trust and respect.

The Flourishing phase is for the organizations that have reached the stage of "Come-Come" and create new companies, i.e. the new business units that have their own products, as well as their own production and marketing capacities. These new units can exist for themselves. Like an adult tree, a company that has reached blossom also contains seeds of new companies in its fruits. They are not just new functions. They are new profit centres. Organization of the Flourishing period is typically a group of profit centres that share some functions for the sake of economies of scale, for the benefit of coordination or for the sake of preserving the critical mass for further creation. Blossoming, is an optimal state of the life cycle, achieving a balance between self-control and flexibility.

Symptoms of the Aging organization emerging from the state of prosperity can be seen in its financial statements. Financial statements also help to detect a disease when abnormal symptoms appear in them, and we can only hope that they saw the problems before they acquired the nature of the pathology. The purpose is to identify the symptoms of impairment when there is still the possibility of preventive treatment of the disease.

At the Aristocracy phase, organizations reduce expectations of growth, show little interest in conquering new markets, mastering new technologies and expanding borders, focus on past achievements rather than future vision; are suspicious of the changes; reward those who do what they are told to do; are more interested in maintaining interpersonal relationships; spend money on control systems and on the arrangement of premises; worry about how to do rather than what and why; require adherence to traditions, and compliance with formalities.

Companies that have reached the Salem City phase have the following characteristics. People focus on who created the problems, not on what to do to solve them. Problems are personified; instead of dealing with the problems of the organization, people are involved in the conflicts, accuse and discredit each other. The organization includes universal paranoia. In the undercover struggle, everyone is included; nobody has time to deal with the needs of the client.

At the phase of Bureaucracy, companies are unable to generate enough resources on their own. They justify their existence by the simple fact that they are of interest to another organization that is ready to provide their support. The organization needs an artificial life support system that allows delaying the Death. And what ensures the provision of such a system is a political decision.

Organizational Death phase typically happens when the lack of resources to reward employees of the organization for their work. The organization is dead when none of its members want to appear at work: there is no reason for this anymore. Death comes at a time when nobody has the commitment of the organization.

The four managerial roles to account for the above phases, are: Purposeful (P), Administrative (A), Entrepreneurial (E) and Integrative (I) (Fig. 5).

8 Large-Scale Organization Management: Adizes Approach

Adizes program teaches "leaders of change" when they need to focus their efforts on external integration when, on the inside, and when in both directions at once [7]. The tools of this systematic approach support the processes of internal, external and internal and external integration. This therapeutic intervention allows analyzing the state of organizations and determining, depending on their position on the life-cycle curve, what is likely to happen (i.e. predicting crises) – see Fig. 5. The Adizes methodology outlines the therapy, depending on the stage of the life cycle, which the organization itself implements [1, 2]. The structure of each organization, its management style, remuneration system, planning process, objectives and other features may be desirable or destructive depending on the organization's position on the life-cycle curve.

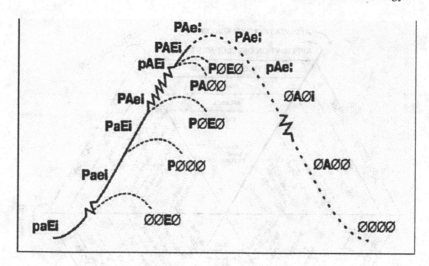

Fig. 5. The Role of Interaction

9 Optimizing Data Management: Enhanced Spiral Model

Every lifecycle stage of the software system development can be optimized. To optimize the lifecycle, i.e. to adapt it for crisis conditions, a complex methodology is required. This complex methodology is a combination of a set of models, methods, CASE tools and practices. The methodology is process-based, and it has six stages, each of which produces certain deliverables in terms of software product components and their connectors. At the most abstract level, these are key concepts of the product and certain relationships between these concepts. Next, high-level architectural modules and interfaces follow [20]. These stages are shown in Fig. 6.

10 Processes, Data, and Systems: The Agility Matrix

Agility is related to balancing business requirements and technology constraints. Many local crises result from misbalancing of these two aspects. Hence, agility is essential in other to achieve a well-balanced software solution. Agility is a remedy for crisis. When a crisis occurs, agility is vital for any kind of business organisation, if it wants to overcome the crisis. Agility should be present in each and every stage of the enterprise system life cycle. In the case of an enterprise, its agility is a concept that incorporates the ideas of "flexibility, balance, adaptability, and coordination under one umbrella" [6, 16]. For each of the perspectives, we identify a set of business management levels, such as strategic decision- making or everyday management. After we combine these perspectives and the business management levels, we get the enterprise agility matrix (Fig. 7); this matrix is a tool for monitoring, predicting and preventing the crises [12].

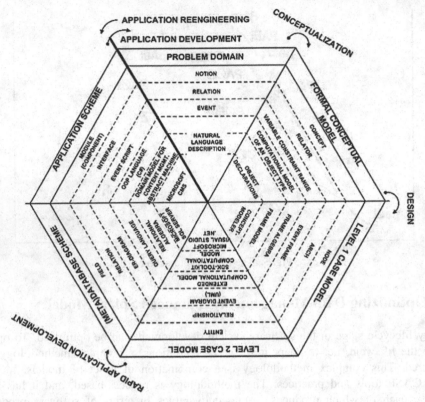

Fig. 6. Optimized spiral model

11 Conclusion

After 50 years, IT crisis, is still a critical issue. To address these crises, a specific discipline is required, and we suggest the IT Crisisology Framework (ITCF) to manage this issue. However, as material and IT product lifecycles are very different, to perform crisis management, there should be a combination of methodology-based optimization (e.g. Agile, SCRUM, XP, OpenUP, ICONIX) and communication [9]. This results in the conquering of crisis as our ITCF approach is combined with software development discipline, knowing that factors determining efficiency and productivity in the short and long term are delivered and integrated according to a predictable model.

Our ITCF approach incorporate the three "pillars" of business, technology and human-related factors (T-, B- and H-factors); it also includes a set of lifecycle-based models. These models include data, process and system related aspects. One aspect of presenting and balancing the above three aspects in crisis is the Agility Matrix; to address data lifecycle specifically, we recommend using the Optimized Spiral Model.

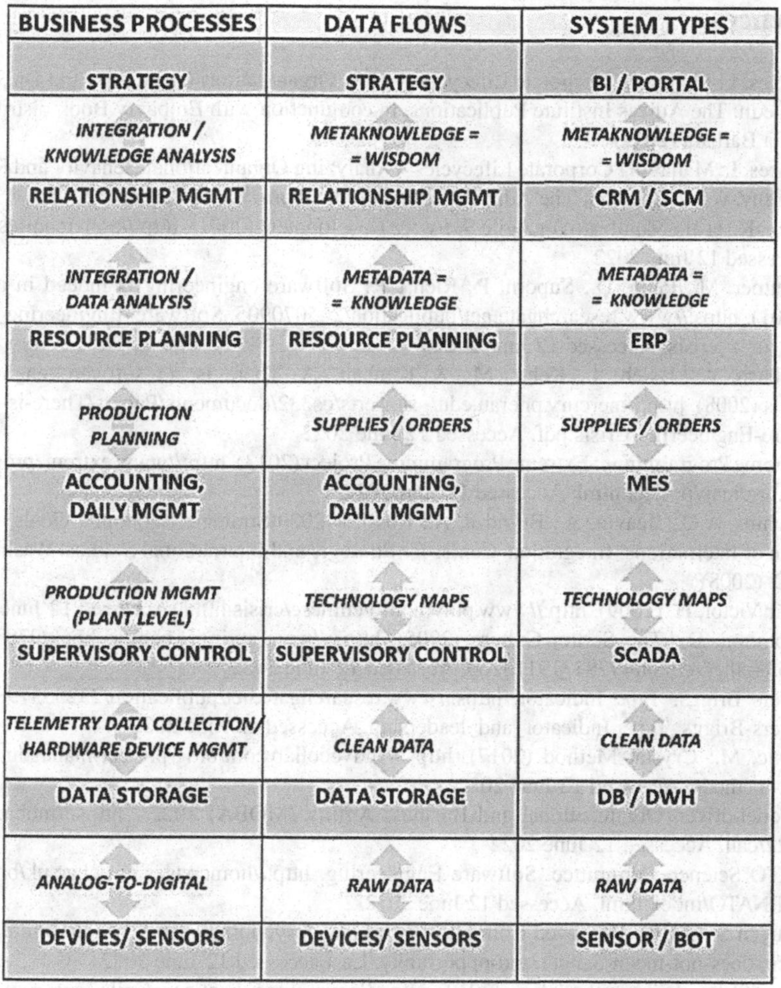

BUSINESS PROCESSES	DATA FLOWS	SYSTEM TYPES
STRATEGY	STRATEGY	BI / PORTAL
INTEGRATION / KNOWLEDGE ANALYSIS	METAKNOWLEDGE = = WISDOM	METAKNOWLEDGE = = WISDOM
RELATIONSHIP MGMT	RELATIONSHIP MGMT	CRM / SCM
INTEGRATION / DATA ANALYSIS	METADATA = = KNOWLEDGE	METADATA = = KNOWLEDGE
RESOURCE PLANNING	RESOURCE PLANNING	ERP
PRODUCTION PLANNING	SUPPLIES / ORDERS	SUPPLIES / ORDERS
ACCOUNTING, DAILY MGMT	ACCOUNTING, DAILY MGMT	MES
PRODUCTION MGMT (PLANT LEVEL)	TECHNOLOGY MAPS	TECHNOLOGY MAPS
SUPERVISORY CONTROL	SUPERVISORY CONTROL	SCADA
TELEMETRY DATA COLLECTION/ HARDWARE DEVICE MGMT	CLEAN DATA	CLEAN DATA
DATA STORAGE	DATA STORAGE	DB / DWH
ANALOG-TO-DIGITAL	RAW DATA	RAW DATA
DEVICES/ SENSORS	DEVICES/ SENSORS	SENSOR / BOT

Fig. 7. Agility matrix

To manage technology (and knowledge) transfer, the authors suggest using enhanced Shannon information model and the "soft skills" tailoring based on the "seven principles". Adizes framework and agile methods are also used to predict crises, and dynamically adjust the "iron" triangle parameters on order to optimize the lifecycle based on mission-critical trade-offs (ACDM/ATAM and SMART methods) [15].

Systemic application of the above-mentioned models, methods, principles and practices under the umbrella of the ITCF methodology results in disciplined, predictable, manageable and adjustable software product development even in case of volatile and uncertain crisis conditions.

References

1. Adizes, I.: Managing Corporate Lifecycles – How Organizations Grow, Age and Die, vol. 1, 2nd edn. The Adizes Institute Publications, in conjunction with Embassy Book distributors, Santa Barbara (2012)
2. Adizes, I.: Managing Corporate Lifecycles – Analyzing Organizational Behavior and Raising Healthy, vol. 2, 2nd edn. The Adizes Institute Publications, Santa Barbara (2015)
3. Beck, K., et al.: Manifesto for Agile Software Development (2001). http://agilemanifesto.org. Accessed 12 June 2022
4. Buettner, M., Peng, D., Suporn, P., Richa, P.: Software engineering is indeed in a crisis (2001). https://www.researchgate.net/publication/265070905_Software_Engineering_is_ind eed_in_a_crisis. Accessed 12 June 2022
5. Colburn, A., Hsieh, J., Kehrt, M., & Kimball, A. There is no software engineering crisis (2008). http://mercury.pr.erau.edu/~siewerts/cs332/documents/Papers/There-is-no-Sof tware-Engineering-Crisis.pdf. Accessed 12 June 2022
6. Extreme Programming: Extreme Programming Project (2013). http://www.extremeprogramm ing.org/map/project.html. Accessed 12 June 2022
7. Kuchins, A.C., Beavin, A., Bryndza, A.: Russia's 2020 Strategic Economic Goals and the Role of International Integration. Center for Strategic and International Studies, Washington, D.C. (2008)
8. Mair Victor, H. (2009). http://www.pinyin.info/chinese/crisis.html. Accessed 12 June 2022
9. Maximini, D.: The Scrum Culture (2005). https://www.springer.com/us/book/978331936 5053#otherversion=9783319118260. Accessed 12 June 2022
10. Myers Briggs. Type Indicator. https://www.researchgate.net/publication/232553798_The_ Myers-Briggs_Type_Indicator_and_leadership. Accessed 12 June 2022
11. Mrsic, M.: Crystal Method (2017). https://activecollab.com/blog/project-management/cry stal-methods. Accessed 12 June 2022
12. "Model-driven Organizational and Business Agility (MOBA) 2022". https://moba.hse.ru/ 2022/call. Accessed 12 June 2022
13. NATO Science Committee. Software Engineering. http://homepages.cs.ncl.ac.uk/brian.ran dell/NATO/index.html. Accessed 12 June 2022
14. Nguyen S. (2014). Retrieved from https://workplacepsychology.net/2014/08/10/in-chinese-crisis-does-not-mean-danger-and-opportunity. Last accessed 12 June 2022
15. Smart Sheet. Agile methodology (2019). https://www.smartsheet.com/agile-vs-scrum-vs-wat erfall-vs-kanban. Accessed 12 June 2022
16. Tutorials Point: Extreme Programming (2019). https://www.tutorialspoint.com/extreme_prog ramming/index.htm. Accessed 12 June 2022
17. Tutorials Point: Agile Methodology (2019). https://www.tutorialspoint.com/agile/index.htm. Accessed 12 June 2022
18. Tutorials Point: Adaptive Software Development (2019). https://www.tutorialspoint.com/ada ptive_software_development. Accessed 12 June 2022
19. Zykov, S.V.: Crisis Management for Software Development and Knowledge Transfer. Issue 61: Springer Series in Smart Innovation, Systems and Technologies, 133 p. Springer, Cham (2016). https://doi.org/10.1007/978-3-319-42966-3
20. Zykov, S.V.: Managing Software Crisis: A Smart Way to Enterprise Agility. Issue 92: Springer Series in Smart Innovation, Systems and Technologies, 153 p. Springer, Cham (2018). https:// doi.org/10.1007/978-3-319-77917-1

Correction to: Proposal for Determining the Angular Position of Artificial Intraocular Lens in the Human Eye

Martin Fus(iD), Josef Pavlicek(iD), Sarka Pitrova(iD), and Michal Hruska(iD)

Correction to:
Chapter "Proposal for Determining the Angular Position of Artificial Intraocular Lens in the Human Eye" in: E. Babkin et al. (Eds.): *Model-Driven Organizational and Business Agility*, LNBIP 457, https://doi.org/10.1007/978-3-031-17728-6_2

In the originally published version of chapter 2, there was an error in the affiliation of the author Michal Hruska. This has been corrected.

The updated original version of this chapter can be found at
https://doi.org/10.1007/978-3-031-17728-6_2

Author Index

Printed in the United States
by Baker & Taylor Publisher Services